W8. BUU. 265

JUN 2 8 2012

THE UNITED STATES CONSTITUTION

THE
UNITED STATES
CONSTITUTION

A GRAPHIC ADAPTATION

WRITTEN BY

JONATHAN HENNESSEY

ART BY

AARON McCONNELL

A NOVEL GRAPHIC from HILL AND WANG

A division of FARRAR, STRAUS AND GIROUX NEW YORK

Hill and Wang
A division of Farrar, Straus and Giroux
18 West 18th Street, New York 10011

Library of Congress Cataloging-in-Publication Data
Hennessey, Jonathan, 1971–
   The United States Constitution : a graphic adaptation / written by Jonathan Hennessey ;
  illustrated by Aaron McConnell.— 1st ed.
     p. cm.
  ISBN-13: 978-0-8090-9487-5 (hardcover : alk. paper)
  ISBN-10: 0-8090-9487-8 (hardcover : alk. paper)
  ISBN-13: 978-0-8090-9470-7 (pbk. : alk. paper)
  ISBN-10: 0-8090-9470-3 (pbk. : alk. paper)
   1. United States. Constitution—Pictorial works. 2. Constitutional history—United
States—Pictorial works. I. McConnell, Aaron, 1976– II. Title.

E303 .H46 2009
320.973—dc22

                                           2008017927

Inking assistance from Steve Lieber, Dennis Culver, and Periscope Studio

Color assistance from Dan McConnell, Cat Ellis, James Ratcliff, and Periscope Studio

Lettering by Jason Arthur

www.fsgbooks.com

10 9 8 7 6

CONTENTS

THE UNITED STATES CONSTITUTION

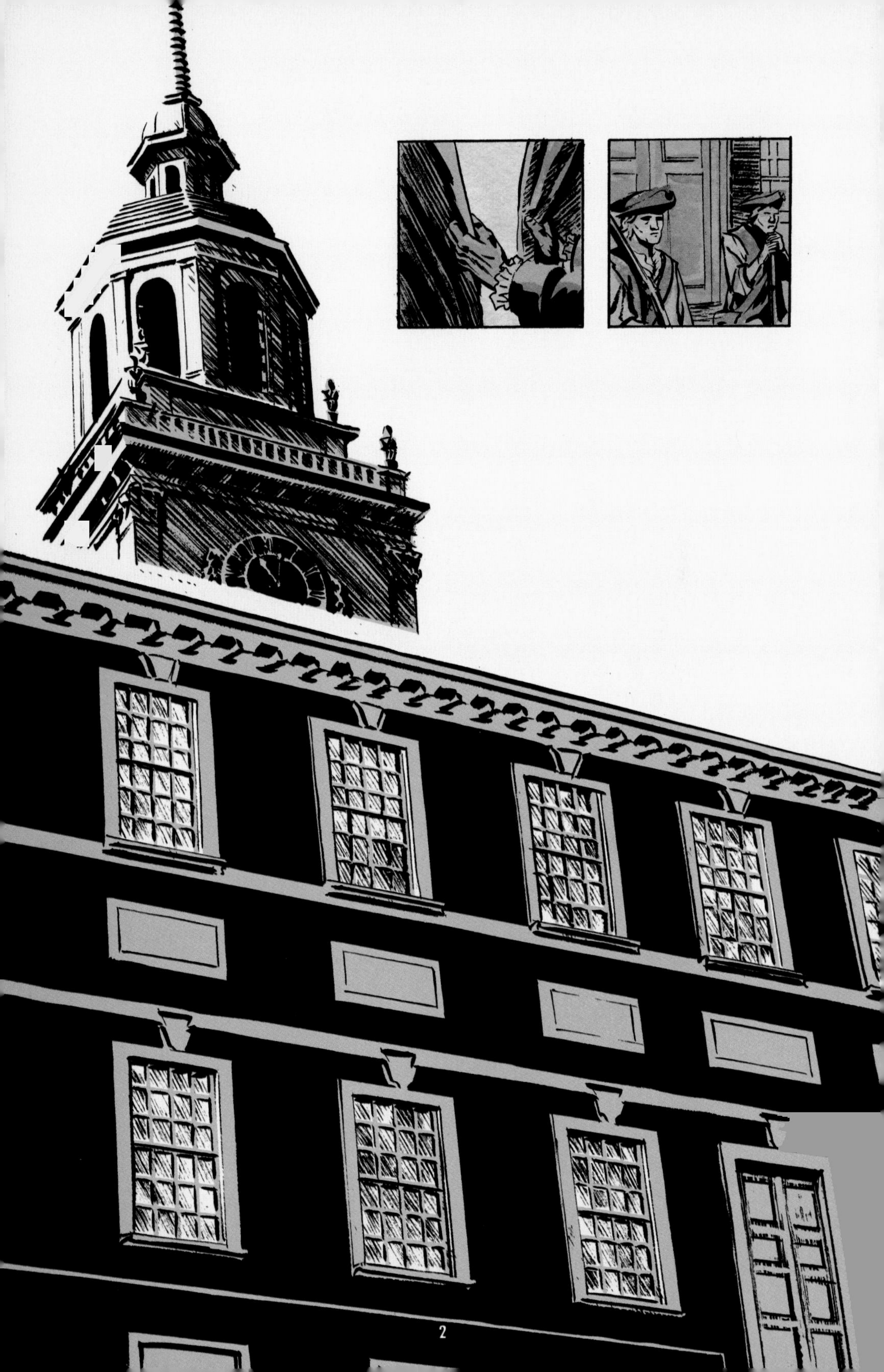

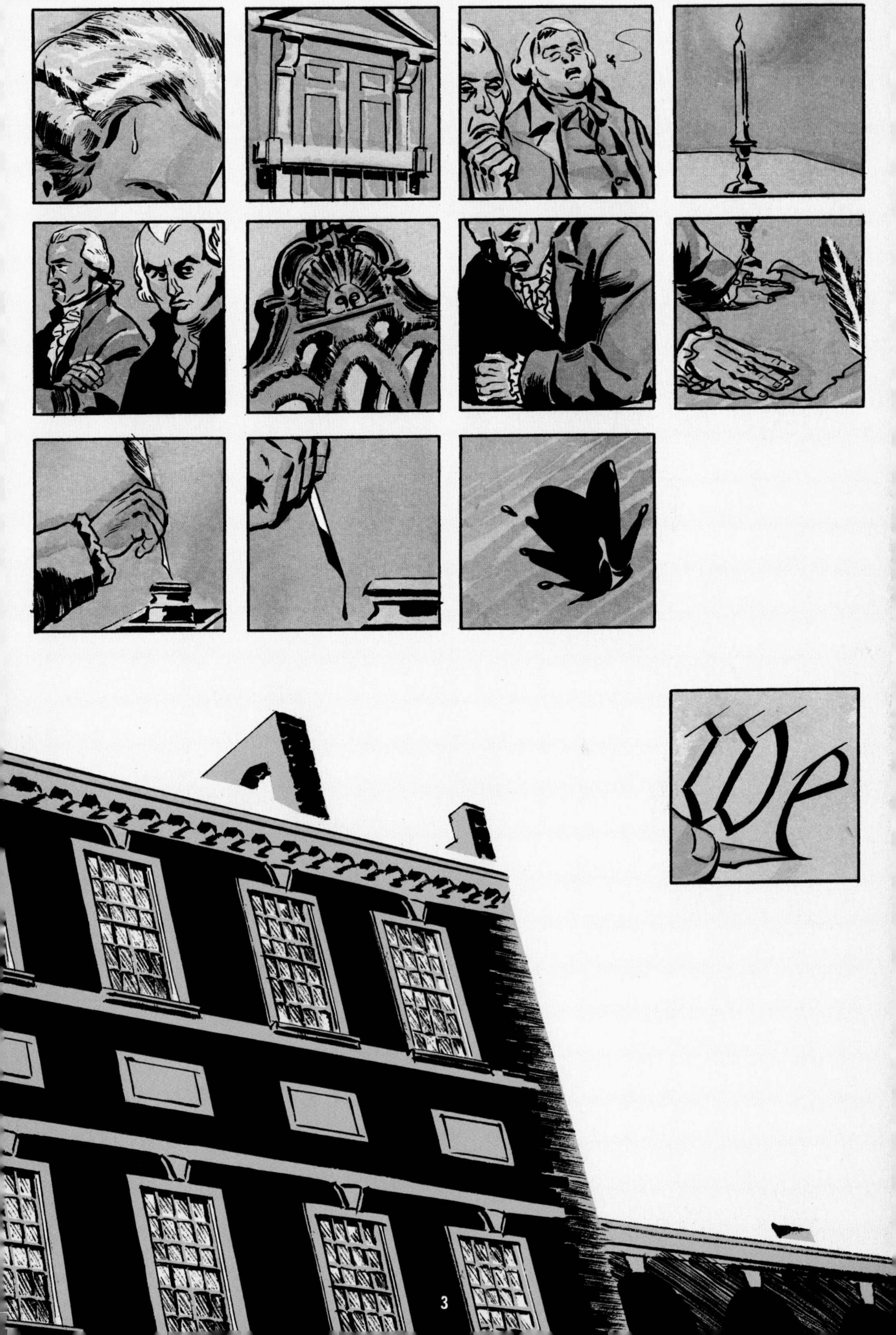
We

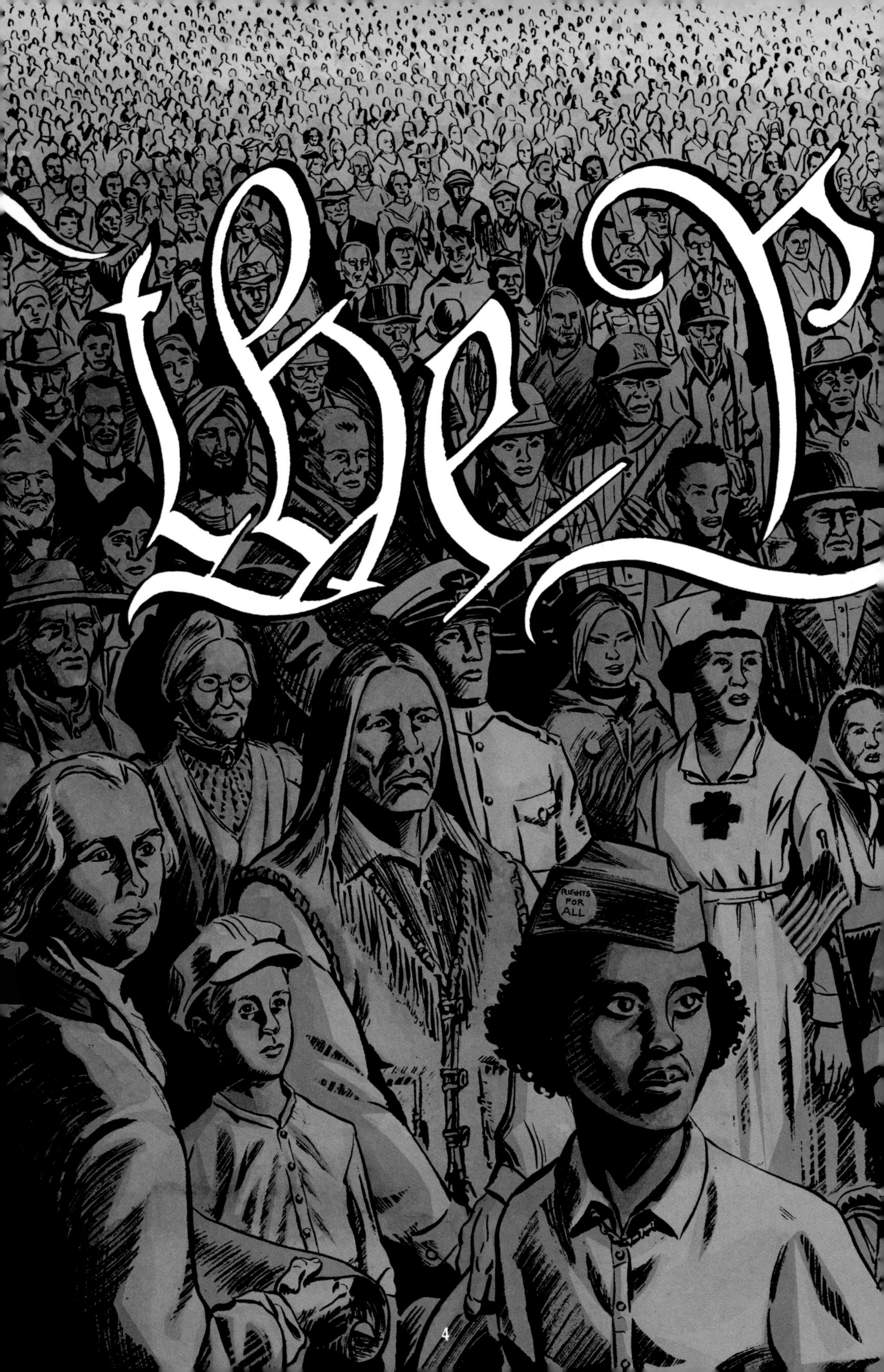
We
RIGHTS FOR ALL

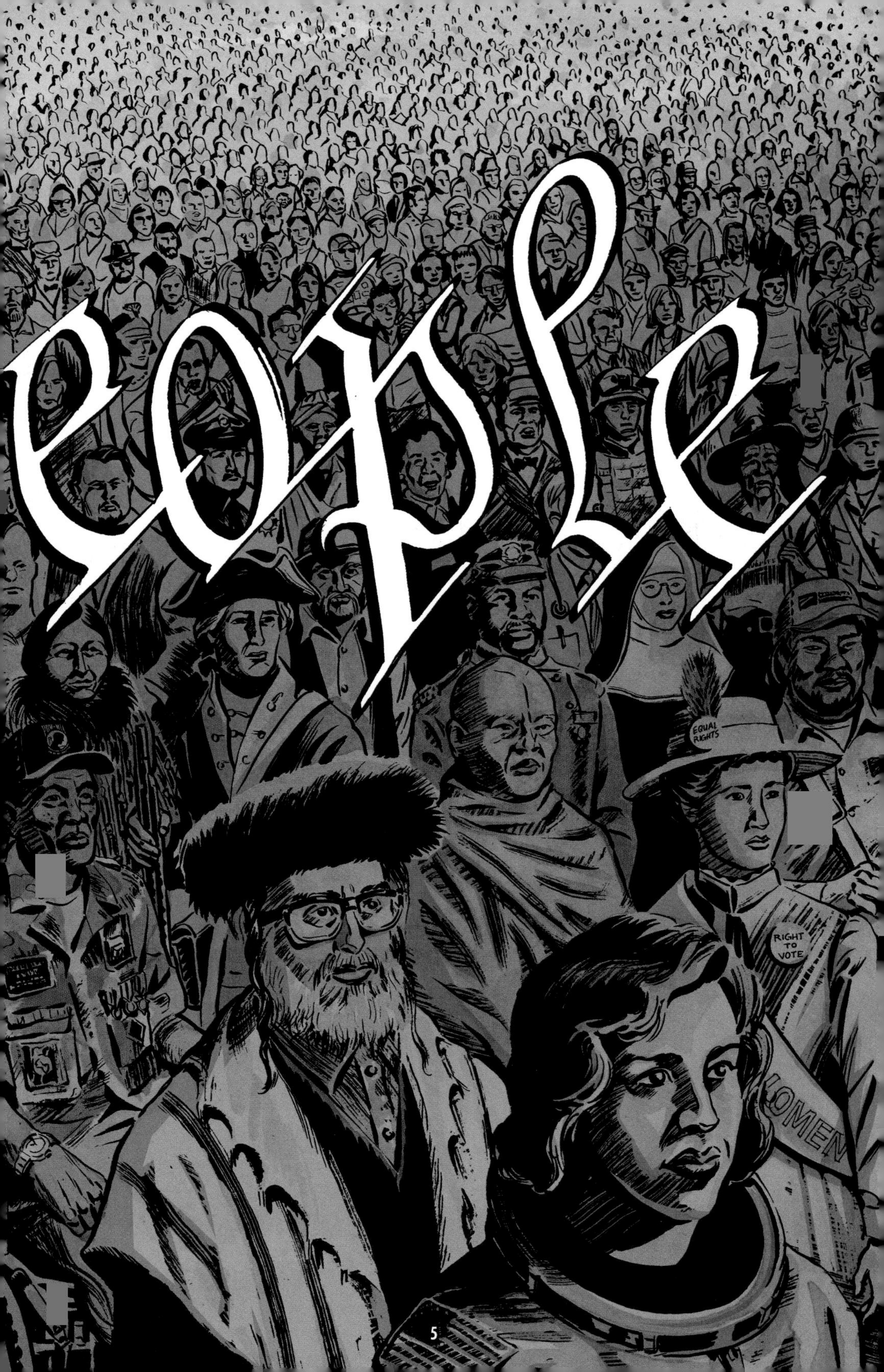
eople
EQUAL RIGHTS
RIGHT TO VOTE
OMEN

BEFORE THERE WAS A CONSTITUTION...

...BEFORE THERE WAS EVEN A UNITED STATES OF AMERICA...

..."WE, THE PEOPLE" WERE A PEOPLE *AT WAR*.

KLIKKLIKKLIK

?

"THE SUMMER SOLDIER AND THE SUNSHINE PATRIOT WILL, IN THIS CRISIS, SHRINK FROM THE SERVICE OF THEIR COUNTRY..."

KLIKKLIKKLIK

"...BUT HE THAT STANDS IT NOW..."

"...DESERVES THE LOVE AND THANKS OF MAN AND WOMAN."

"TYRANNY, LIKE HELL, IS NOT EASILY CONQUERED, YET WE HAVE THIS CONSOLATION WITH US, THAT THE HARDER THE CONFLICT, THE MORE GLORIOUS THE TRIUMPH."

THEN THE WHOLE OF AMERICA WAS JUST A FEW MILLION PEOPLE SCATTERED ACROSS THIRTEEN COLONIES.

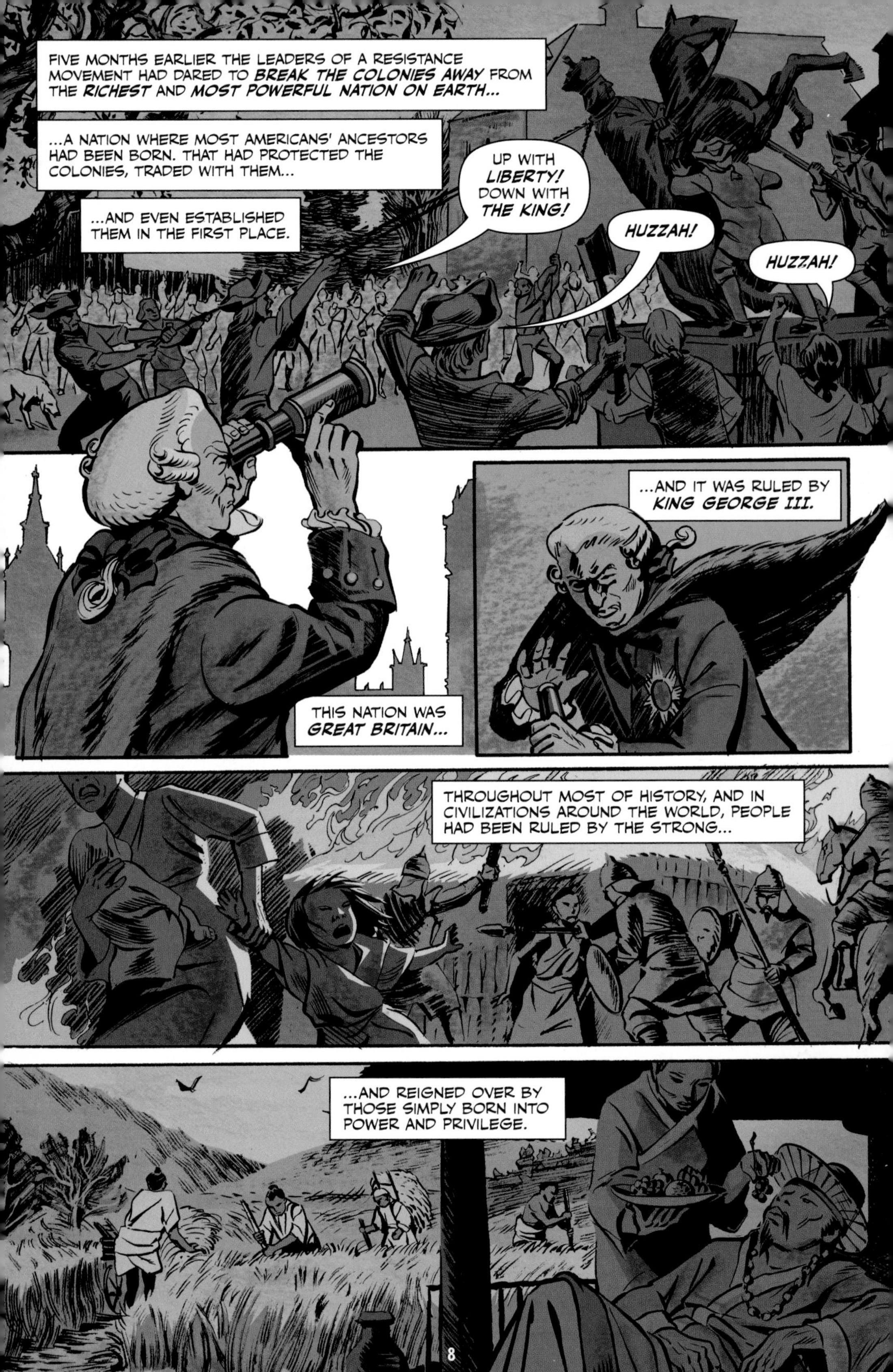

FIVE MONTHS EARLIER THE LEADERS OF A RESISTANCE MOVEMENT HAD DARED TO ***BREAK THE COLONIES AWAY*** FROM THE ***RICHEST*** AND ***MOST POWERFUL NATION ON EARTH...***
...A NATION WHERE MOST AMERICANS' ANCESTORS HAD BEEN BORN. THAT HAD PROTECTED THE COLONIES, TRADED WITH THEM...
...AND EVEN ESTABLISHED THEM IN THE FIRST PLACE.
UP WITH ***LIBERTY!*** DOWN WITH ***THE KING!***
HUZZAH!
HUZZAH!
THIS NATION WAS ***GREAT BRITAIN...***
...AND IT WAS RULED BY ***KING GEORGE III.***
THROUGHOUT MOST OF HISTORY, AND IN CIVILIZATIONS AROUND THE WORLD, PEOPLE HAD BEEN RULED BY THE STRONG...
...AND REIGNED OVER BY THOSE SIMPLY BORN INTO POWER AND PRIVILEGE.

FEW EVEN QUESTIONED THAT THE RIGHT OF RULERS TO RULE CAME FROM ON HIGH.

YET GREAT THINKERS HAD CONTEMPLATED HUMANKIND'S TENDENCY TO SURRENDER TO ITS WORST IMPULSES OF *GREED, FEAR, VIOLENCE,* AND *LUST FOR POWER...*

NOR DID THEY CHALLENGE THAT IT WAS THE PLACE OF THE PEOPLE TO OBEY.

...AND BY THE 1800S THEY HAD LEFT THEIR MARK ON THE WESTERN WORLD.

ADVANCES IN SCIENCE AND MATHEMATICS WERE TRANSFORMING THE WAY EDUCATED PEOPLE LOOKED AT THE UNIVERSE...

...AND WERE BRINGING A NEW UNDERSTANDING AND RESPECT FOR THE LAWS OF NATURE AND THE POWER OF HUMAN REASON.

A CENTURY OF POLITICAL AND RELIGIOUS TURMOIL IN BRITAIN AND EUROPE INSPIRED NEW IDEAS ABOUT THE BEST WAYS FOR HUMAN BEINGS TO LIVE TOGETHER IN PEACE.

9

REJECTING THE NOTION THAT CIVILIZATION AND ITS STRUCTURE ARE PREORDAINED BY GOD...

...PHILOSOPHERS SUCH AS *JOHN LOCKE* ARGUED INSTEAD THAT THEY ARE CHOSEN BY THE PEOPLE.

LOCKE HELD THAT ALL MEN ARE CREATED EQUAL, WITH NATURAL-BORN RIGHTS TO *LIFE, LIBERTY, AND PROPERTY*...

...AND THAT THESE RIGHTS ARE ALWAYS IN JEOPARDY UNLESS PEOPLE COMPROMISE THEIR ABSOLUTE FREEDOM AND FORM LAW-ABIDING *GOVERNMENTS* UNDER WHICH TO LIVE.

GOVERNMENT, THEN, IS LEGITIMATE ONLY IF IT IS BY THE *CONSENT OF THE MAJORITY OF THE PEOPLE*...

...AND ITS POWER MUST NOT BE *ABSOLUTE.* GOVERNMENT MUST BE *LIMITED* TO POWERS THAT THE PEOPLE HAVE GIVEN IT AND THAT SERVE THE PUBLIC GOOD.

WITH ITS OPENING PHRASE, THE CONSTITUTION BOLDLY AFFIRMS THAT THE SOURCE OF ALL GOVERNMENT POWER IS FROM THE PEOPLE, AND ONLY THE PEOPLE.

IN GREAT BRITAIN HIS IDEAS WERE SO RADICAL THAT LOCKE, FEARING FOR HIS LIFE, NEVER ADMITTED HE WAS THEIR AUTHOR UNTIL SHORTLY BEFORE HIS DEATH.

BUT IN THE AMERICAN COLONIES...

...THEY HELPED START A REVOLUTION.

IT WAS MORE THAN JUST A CLASH OF IDEAS THAT SPARKED THE *AMERICAN REVOLUTION,* HOWEVER.

THANKS TO THE MONTHS-LONG PERILOUS OCEAN VOYAGE THAT SEPARATED THEM FROM LONDON...

THE ATLANTIC OCEAN

THE ATLANTIC OCEAN

T H E

T I

...FOR DECADES, THE COLONIES HAD PRACTICALLY GOVERNED THEMSELVES.

BUT GEORGE III AND THE *BRITISH PARLIAMENT* NEEDED MONEY NOT ONLY TO FUND THEIR WAR IN EUROPE...

...BUT ALSO TO SUPPORT THE BRITISH TROOPS IN AMERICA THAT HAD PUSHED THE FRENCH WEST OF THE MISSISSIPPI AND HELPED PROTECT THE COLONISTS FROM NATIVE AMERICANS.

THE BRITISH CRACKED DOWN ON THE COLONIES WITH THE PASSAGE OF RESTRICTIVE LAWS AND TAXES, LIKE THE 1765 *STAMP ACT*.

"THAT PROVISION BE MADE FOR RAISING A FURTHER REVENUE WITHIN YOUR MAJESTY'S DOMINIONS IN AMERICA"...

..."WE, YOUR MAJESTY'S MOST DUTIFUL AND LOYAL SUBJECTS"...

..."GRANT UNTO YOUR MAJESTY THE SEVERAL RATES AND DUTIES HEREIN AFTER MENTIONED."

NO TAXATION WITHOUT REPRESENTATION!

HEAR! HEAR!

FOLLY OF ENGLAND

TO MANY COLONISTS, PARLIAMENT'S TAMPERING WITH THEIR LIVELIHOOD AND LOCAL AFFAIRS WITH LAWS AND TAXES WAS UNACCEPTABLE.

AND TO MOST IN PARLIAMENT, THE GALL OF THE AMERICANS TO DEFY THEM WAS JUST AS MUCH OF AN OUTRAGE.

"THAT THE SAID COLONIES AND PLANTATIONS IN AMERICA HAVE BEEN, ARE, AND OF RIGHT OUGHT TO BE, SUBORDINATE UNTO, AND DEPENDENT UPON THE IMPERIAL CROWN AND PARLIAMENT OF GREAT BRITAIN"...

..."AND THAT THE KING'S MAJESTY"...

..."HAD, HATH, AND OF RIGHT OUGHT TO HAVE, FULL POWER AND AUTHORITY TO MAKE LAWS AND STATUTES OF SUFFICIENT FORCE AND VALIDITY TO BIND THE COLONIES AND PEOPLE OF AMERICA, SUBJECTS OF THE CROWN OF GREAT BRITAIN, IN ALL CASES WHATSOEVER."

OVER THE NEXT DECADE PARLIAMENT AND THE KING WRESTLED BITTERLY WITH THE GROWING REBELLION.

RIOTS, BOYCOTTING BRITISH GOODS, DECLARATION OF RIGHTS AND GRIEVANCES

TOWNSHEND ACTS, REVENUE ACTS, INTOLERABLE ACTS

UHHHNNH...!

MMMPPHHH...!

THE UNITED STATES OF AMERICA

2

2

TWO DOLLARS

Free and Independent States

AS TENSIONS ROSE, *THE CONTINENTAL CONGRESS*— A GATHERING OF PATRIOTS LIKE *THOMAS JEFFERSON*— DRAFTED THE DECLARATION OF INDEPENDENCE.

WITH IT, THE COLONIES DARED BREAK AWAY FROM BRITAIN.

SETTING THE STAGE FOR A BLOODY FIVE-YEAR WAR...

...AND PITTING A TINY FORCE OF AMERICAN REBELS AGAINST THE MIGHTIEST MILITARY IN THE WORLD.

GEN. *GEORGE WASHINGTON* HAD NO NAVY AND FEW HEAVY WEAPONS. AND HIS SOLDIERS WERE BARELY MORE THAN AN UNDISCIPLINED MOB.

BY MOST COUNTS, WASHINGTON WON ONLY TWO BATTLES IN THE ENTIRE *REVOLUTIONARY WAR.*

BUT FRANCE'S MONEY, NAVY, AND MANPOWER CAME TO HIS AID. AND WITH THE BRITISH BOGGED DOWN IN FIGHTING CLOSER TO HOME...

...WASHINGTON DIDN'T SO MUCH HAVE TO WIN. HE JUST HAD NOT TO LOSE.

THIS WAS STILL A BACKBREAKING, HIGH-STAKES TASK. AND MANY TIMES DEFEAT LOOKED ALL BUT CERTAIN.

THE AMERICAN VICTORY WAS BY THE SKIN OF THEIR TEETH.

NOW THE COLONIES HAD THEIR FREEDOM.

SSSTT

PUFF

SO, WHAT WOULD THEY DO WITH IT?

THE ANSWER?

FIGHT AMONG THEMSELVES.

in Order to form a more perfect Union

WITH THESE WORDS, THE CONSTITUTION REFERS TO A UNION AMONG THE FORMER COLONIES THAT ACTUALLY CAME *BEFORE* THE UNITED STATES OF AMERICA WAS OFFICIALLY FORMED.

AND THAT UNION—WHILE A LEAP FORWARD FOR THE PEOPLE FROM THE ARBITRARY RULE OF KINGS AND QUEENS—WAS FAR LESS THAN PERFECT.

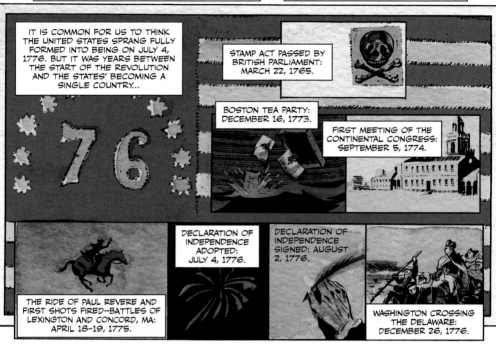

IT IS COMMON FOR US TO THINK THE UNITED STATES SPRANG FULLY FORMED INTO BEING ON JULY 4, 1776. BUT IT WAS YEARS BETWEEN THE START OF THE REVOLUTION AND THE STATES' BECOMING A SINGLE COUNTRY...

STAMP ACT PASSED BY BRITISH PARLIAMENT: MARCH 22, 1765.

BOSTON TEA PARTY: DECEMBER 16, 1773.

FIRST MEETING OF THE CONTINENTAL CONGRESS: SEPTEMBER 5, 1774.

DECLARATION OF INDEPENDENCE ADOPTED: JULY 4, 1776.

DECLARATION OF INDEPENDENCE SIGNED: AUGUST 2, 1776.

THE RIDE OF PAUL REVERE AND FIRST SHOTS FIRED—BATTLES OF LEXINGTON AND CONCORD, MA: APRIL 18-19, 1775.

WASHINGTON CROSSING THE DELAWARE: DECEMBER 26, 1776.

WINTER AT VALLEY FORGE BEGUN: DECEMBER 19, 1777.

BENEDICT ARNOLD DISCOVERED TO BE A TRAITOR: SEPTEMBER 25, 1780.

BRITISH SURRENDER AT YORKTOWN, VA: OCTOBER 19, 1781.

PEACE TREATY SIGNED IN PARIS: SEPTEMBER 3, 1783.

...AND IT WOULD STILL BE 5½ MORE YEARS BEFORE A GOVERNMENT UNDER THE CONSTITUTION OF THE UNITED STATES WAS ACTUALLY UP AND RUNNING.

REMEMBER, THE COLONIES HAD HAD NO CONSTITUTION OR PRESIDENT DURING THE REVOLUTION OR EVEN IMMEDIATELY AFTER IT.

INSTEAD, THE FORMER COLONIES—NOW CALLING THEMSELVES *STATES*—HAD MADE AN AGREEMENT CALLED *THE ARTICLES OF CONFEDERATION* TO BIND THEM LOOSELY TOGETHER.

FAR FROM BEING "ONE NATION, INDIVISIBLE," THE STATES WERE LIKE SEPARATE COUNTRIES IN A LEAGUE OF FRIENDSHIP.

Drafting the Articles of Confederation

York Town Pennsylvania 1777 13c USA

THE EXPRESSION *"TOO MANY COOKS SPOIL THE POT"* GIVES A GOOD SENSE OF WHAT AMERICA WAS LIKE UNDER THE ARTICLES OF CONFEDERATION.

THERE WAS A VERY WEAK GOVERNMENT THAT CONSISTED ENTIRELY OF A SINGLE *BRANCH,* THE *CONFEDERATION CONGRESS.*

THE CONFEDERATION CONGRESS WAS SET UP TO PERFORM A LIMITED SET OF TASKS. THESE INCLUDED HELPING SETTLE DISPUTES AMONG THE STATES, REPRESENTING THEM IN FOREIGN AFFAIRS, AND CREATING A MILITARY ALLIANCE.

EACH STATE SEATED BETWEEN TWO AND SEVEN MEMBERS OF CONGRESS. AND NO MATTER WHAT ITS SIZE, POPULATION, OR ECONOMIC POWER, EACH STATE RECEIVED A SINGLE VOTE ON EVERY ISSUE.

THIS ARRANGEMENT ALLOWED VERY SMALL STATES TO OBSTRUCT EASILY THE PROCESS OF PASSING LAWS.

DONT TREAD ON ME

JUST AS DURING THE REVOLUTIONARY WAR WASHINGTON HAD HAD TO TAKE ORDERS FROM A CHORUS OF SOMETIMES CONFLICTING VOICES...

...THE CONFEDERATION CONGRESS HAD NO *EXECUTIVE AUTHORITY* TO HOLD THE STATES TO THEIR DECISIONS OR OBLIGATIONS.

AND SO THINGS IN THIS NEWLY FREE LAND...

...FELL APART FAST.

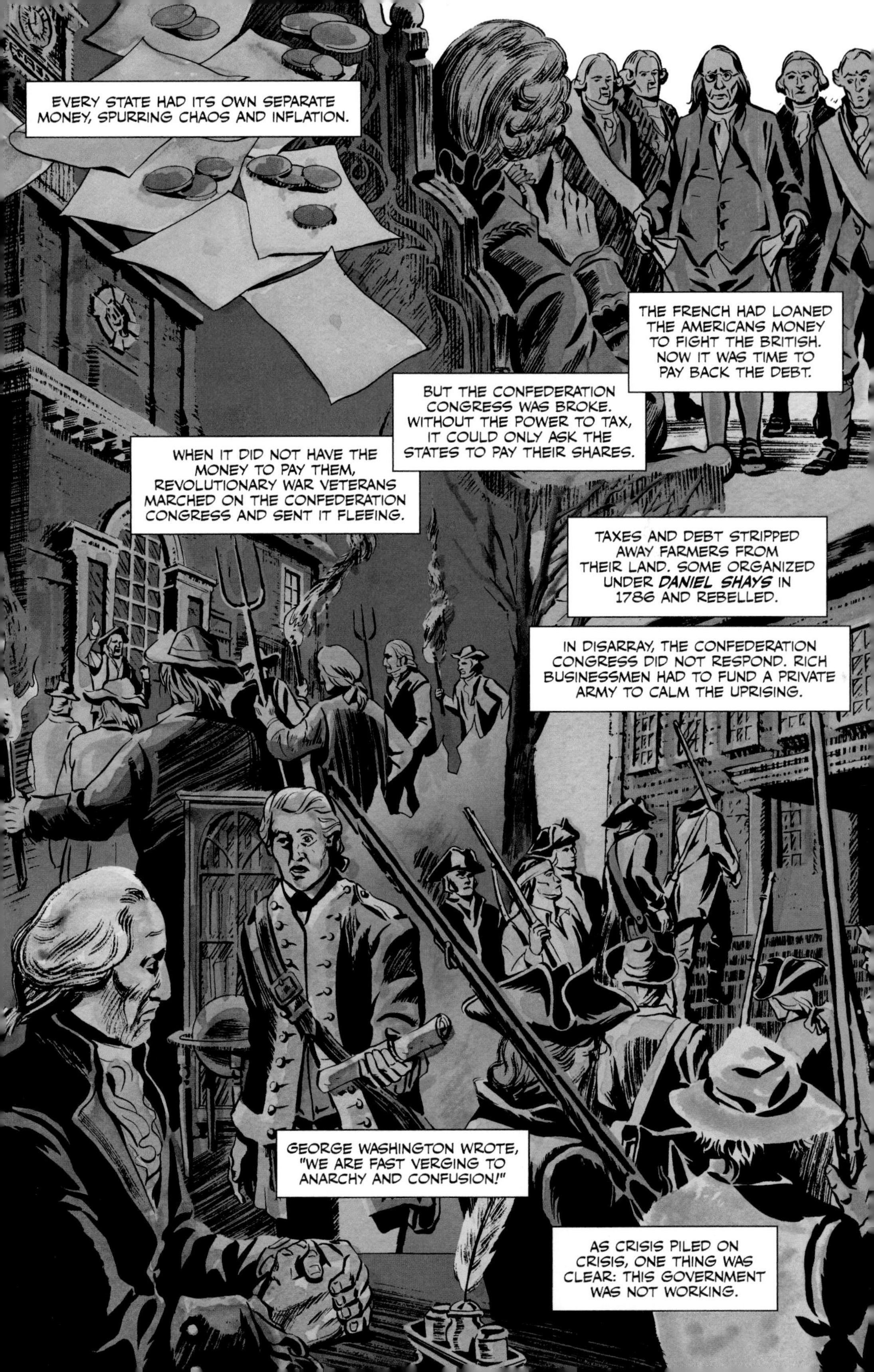
EVERY STATE HAD ITS OWN SEPARATE MONEY, SPURRING CHAOS AND INFLATION.
THE FRENCH HAD LOANED THE AMERICANS MONEY TO FIGHT THE BRITISH. NOW IT WAS TIME TO PAY BACK THE DEBT.
BUT THE CONFEDERATION CONGRESS WAS BROKE. WITHOUT THE POWER TO TAX, IT COULD ONLY ASK THE STATES TO PAY THEIR SHARES.
WHEN IT DID NOT HAVE THE MONEY TO PAY THEM, REVOLUTIONARY WAR VETERANS MARCHED ON THE CONFEDERATION CONGRESS AND SENT IT FLEEING.
TAXES AND DEBT STRIPPED AWAY FARMERS FROM THEIR LAND. SOME ORGANIZED UNDER *DANIEL SHAYS* IN 1786 AND REBELLED.
IN DISARRAY, THE CONFEDERATION CONGRESS DID NOT RESPOND. RICH BUSINESSMEN HAD TO FUND A PRIVATE ARMY TO CALM THE UPRISING.
GEORGE WASHINGTON WROTE, "WE ARE FAST VERGING TO ANARCHY AND CONFUSION!"
AS CRISIS PILED ON CRISIS, ONE THING WAS CLEAR: THIS GOVERNMENT WAS NOT WORKING.

SO IN THE HOT, HUMID SUMMER OF 1787 THE STATES* SENT REPRESENTATIVES TO PHILADELPHIA TO FIND A WAY TO REESTABLISH ORDER.

*ALL EXCEPT RHODE ISLAND.

GEORGE WASHINGTON HAD STUNNED THE WORLD BY LAYING DOWN HIS SWORD AFTER THE WAR. IT HAS BEEN REMARKED THAT OTHER MEN WOULD HAVE SEIZED THE OPPORTUNITY TO MAKE THEMSELVES MILITARY DICTATORS OR KINGS.

THOUGH RETIRED TO COUNTRY LIFE, HE AGREED TO BE PRESIDENT OF THE GATHERING.

SO IN ORDER FOR THE DELEGATES TO "FORM A MORE PERFECT UNION," EVERYTHING ABOUT THE OLD ONE WOULD BE REEXAMINED.

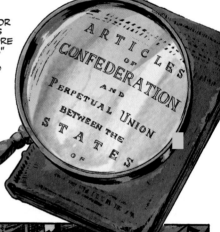

ARTICLES OF CONFEDERATION AND PERPETUAL UNION BETWEEN THE STATES OF

THE BIG PROBLEM WAS POWER: HOW MUCH THERE SHOULD BE, WHO SHOULD WIELD IT, AND HOW TO MINIMIZE ITS CORRUPTING INFLUENCE ON THOSE IN POSITIONS OF LEADERSHIP.

PLACING ALL THE RESPONSIBILITIES OF NATIONAL GOVERNMENT WITHIN THE POWER OF A SINGLE BODY—WHETHER THE CONFEDERATION CONGRESS OR THE BRITISH MONARCHY—HAD FAILED TO SECURE LIBERTY AND SECURITY FOR THE AMERICANS.

SO A "MORE PERFECT UNION" WOULD ESTABLISH A *SEPARATION OF POWERS.*

THIS WOULD PLACE AUTHORITY INTO NOT ONE, BUT THREE BRANCHES OF GOVERNMENT...

...EACH DOING SOME JOBS OF GOVERNMENT...

...BUT NOT OTHERS.

CRANK CRANK CRANK

CRANK

CRANK CRANK

CRANK

TO INSURE THAT NO BRANCH'S POWER COULD SURPASS THAT OF THE OTHERS AND SLIDE THE COUNTRY INTO A TYRANNY THREATENING THE CHERISHED VALUES OF LIFE, LIBERTY, AND PROPERTY...

19

...A SYSTEM OF *CHECKS AND BALANCES* WOULD FORCE THEM TO EXERCISE THEIR INDIVIDUAL POWERS ONLY WITH THE COOPERATION AND, IN SOME CASES, THE PERMISSION OF THE OTHERS.

IN OTHER WORDS, EACH BRANCH BOTH DEPENDS ON THE OTHER TWO AND HAS MULTIPLE WAYS OF CHALLENGING AND RESTRAINING THEIR POWER.

THESE IDEAS, ENVISIONED IN PART BY THE FRENCH PHILOSOPHER *CHARLES DE SECONDAT, BARON MONTESQUIEU*...

...WOULD HELP ELEVATE THE SUPREMACY OF "WE, THE PEOPLE" OVER GOVERNMENT IN PRACTICE AS WELL AS IN WORDS.

WITH ITS WEAK CENTRAL GOVERNMENT, THE ARTICLES OF CONFEDERATION LEFT THE STATES TOO STRONG.

SOUTH CAROLINA STATE BIRD

NEW YORK STATE BIRD

BLUEBIRD

MARYLAND STATE BIRD

BALTIMORE

ORIOLE

GREAT CAROLIN. WREN

THE STATES RETAINED TOO MANY POWERS THAT A NATIONAL GOVERNMENT SHOULD HAVE AND NO BINDING, HIGHER AUTHORITY OVER THEM.

BUT REMEMBER, EVEN AT THE TIME OF THE REVOLUTION, MANY OF THE FORMER COLONIES HAD HAD THEIR OWN CONTINUOUS GOVERNMENTS FOR WELL OVER A HUNDRED YEARS.

AMERICANS HIGHLY VALUED THESE ASSEMBLIES. THERE WOULD BE NO ELIMINATING THEM.

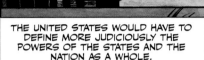

AND THE PEOPLE OF AMERICA HAD JUST FOUGHT A COSTLY WAR WITH ONE POWERFUL GOVERNMENT. WERE THEY READY TO BE RULED BY ANOTHER ONE?

TO MANY, HAVING THEIR OWN LOCAL STATE GOVERNMENT WAS PLENTY.

THE UNITED STATES WOULD HAVE TO DEFINE MORE JUDICIOUSLY THE POWERS OF THE STATES AND THE NATION AS A WHOLE.

THIS ADDED LEVEL OF SEPARATION OF POWERS—A CENTRAL GOVERNMENT DOING SOME JOBS, AND LOCAL GOVERNMENTS, OTHERS—IS KNOWN AS *FEDERALISM*.

IT BECAME THE QUESTION OF HOW TO REALIZE ALL THESE PRINCIPLES THAT THE FOUNDING FATHERS PUT TO THEMSELVES IN THE SECRET SESSIONS OF THE *CONSTITUTIONAL CONVENTION*.

IT WASN'T WHAT THEY HAD BEEN SENT TO DO. AND NOT ALL AGREED THAT THEY SHOULD.

BUT THESE MEN DECIDED TO THROW *OUT* THE DEFECTIVE ARTICLES OF CONFEDERATION...

...AND REPLACE THEM WITH THE CONSTITUTION OF THE UNITED STATES OF AMERICA.

THE CONSTITUTION IS NOT JUST A DOCUMENT; IT IS ALSO AN ACT.

...AN ACT OF CREATING—OF "CONSTITUTING"—13 SEPARATE ENTITIES INTO A NEW, SINGLE COUNTRY.

THE CONSTITUTION IS FAR MORE THAN A SIMPLE LIST OF RIGHTS.

DO-IT-YOURSELF KIT: THE UNITED STATES of AMERICA

ASSEMBLY and INSTALLATION

IT ACTUALLY SETS UP HOW EVERY ASPECT OF OUR GOVERNMENT—OUR COUNTRY—WORKS.

THE IDEA OF CONSTITUTIONS HAD BEEN AROUND SINCE ANCIENT TIMES...

PEOPLE OF ATHENS!

I GIVE YOU YOUR LAWS!

...AND THE INDIVIDUAL STATES HAD BEEN DRAWING UP THEIR OWN SINCE BEFORE INDEPENDENCE.

BACK IN ENGLAND, THERE HAD BEEN A VAGUE CONSTITUTION COLLECTING THE RIGHTS OF THE PEOPLE AND PROCEDURES OF GOVERNMENT...

...BUT THE ENGLISH CONSTITUTION HAD NEVER BEEN WRITTEN DOWN...

...AND THAT DEEPLY TROUBLED THE FRAMERS.

POP

THEIR LAWS—FOR THEIR PEOPLE—WOULD BE IN BLACK AND WHITE...FOR ALL TO SEE... AND FOR THE COMMON GOOD.

BUT ASK 55 FOUNDING FATHERS WHAT THE "COMMON GOOD" ACTUALLY IS...

YEA!

NAY!

...AND YOU WOULD GET 55 DIFFERENT ANSWERS.

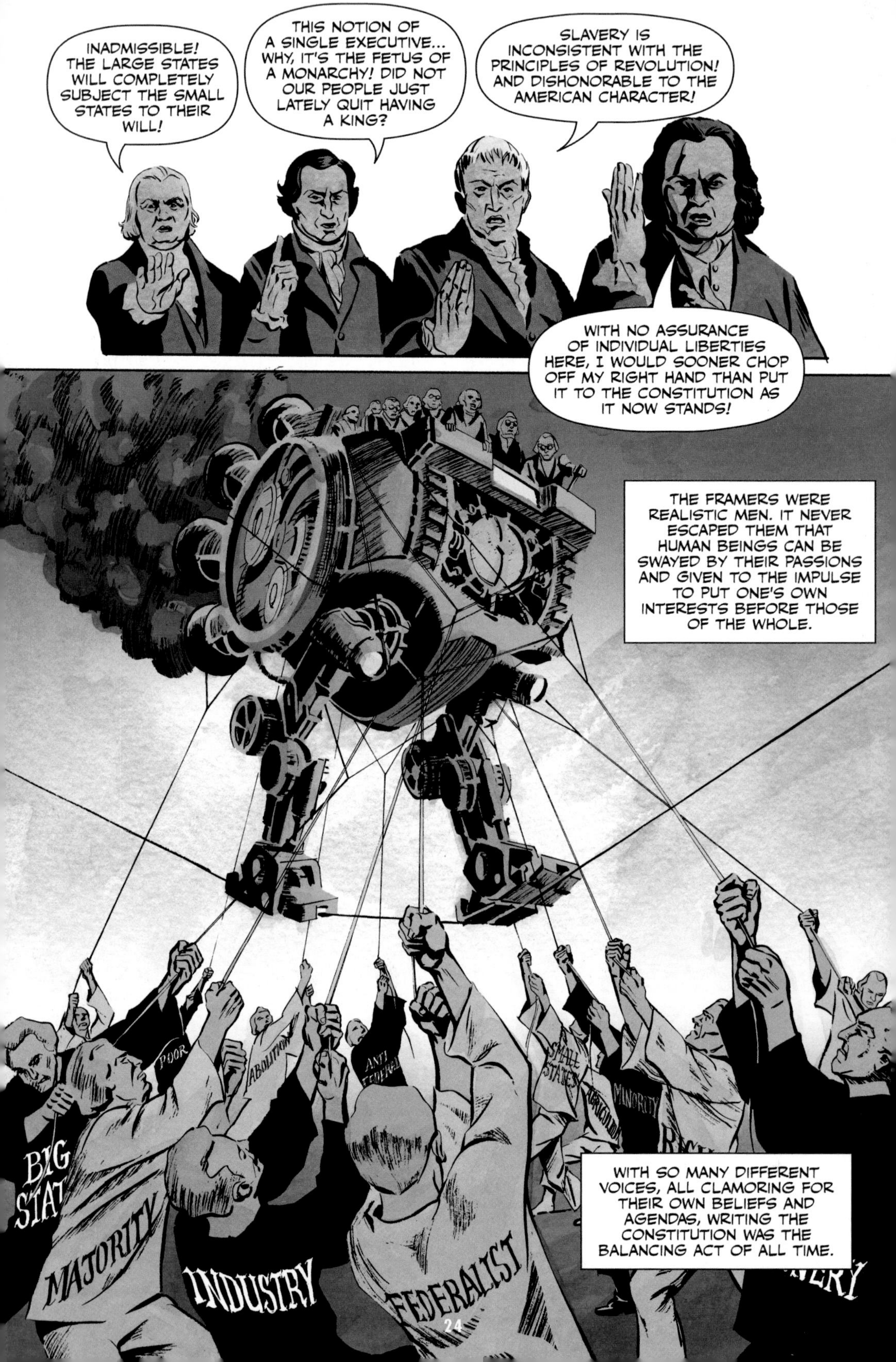
INADMISSIBLE! THE LARGE STATES WILL COMPLETELY SUBJECT THE SMALL STATES TO THEIR WILL!
THIS NOTION OF A SINGLE EXECUTIVE... WHY, IT'S THE FETUS OF A MONARCHY! DID NOT OUR PEOPLE JUST LATELY QUIT HAVING A KING?
SLAVERY IS INCONSISTENT WITH THE PRINCIPLES OF REVOLUTION! AND DISHONORABLE TO THE AMERICAN CHARACTER!
WITH NO ASSURANCE OF INDIVIDUAL LIBERTIES HERE, I WOULD SOONER CHOP OFF MY RIGHT HAND THAN PUT IT TO THE CONSTITUTION AS IT NOW STANDS!
THE FRAMERS WERE REALISTIC MEN. IT NEVER ESCAPED THEM THAT HUMAN BEINGS CAN BE SWAYED BY THEIR PASSIONS AND GIVEN TO THE IMPULSE TO PUT ONE'S OWN INTERESTS BEFORE THOSE OF THE WHOLE.
POOR
ABOLITION
ANTI FEDERAL
SMALL STATES
MINORITY
WITH SO MANY DIFFERENT VOICES, ALL CLAMORING FOR THEIR OWN BELIEFS AND AGENDAS, WRITING THE CONSTITUTION WAS THE BALANCING ACT OF ALL TIME.
MAJORITY
INDUSTRY
FEDERALIST

Preamble

THE REMAINDER OF THIS FIRST PART OF THE CONSTITUTION—THE ***PREAMBLE***—ANSWERS THE QUESTION OF WHAT THE *JOB* OF THE NATIONAL GOVERNMENT OF THE UNITED STATES IS IN THE FIRST PLACE.

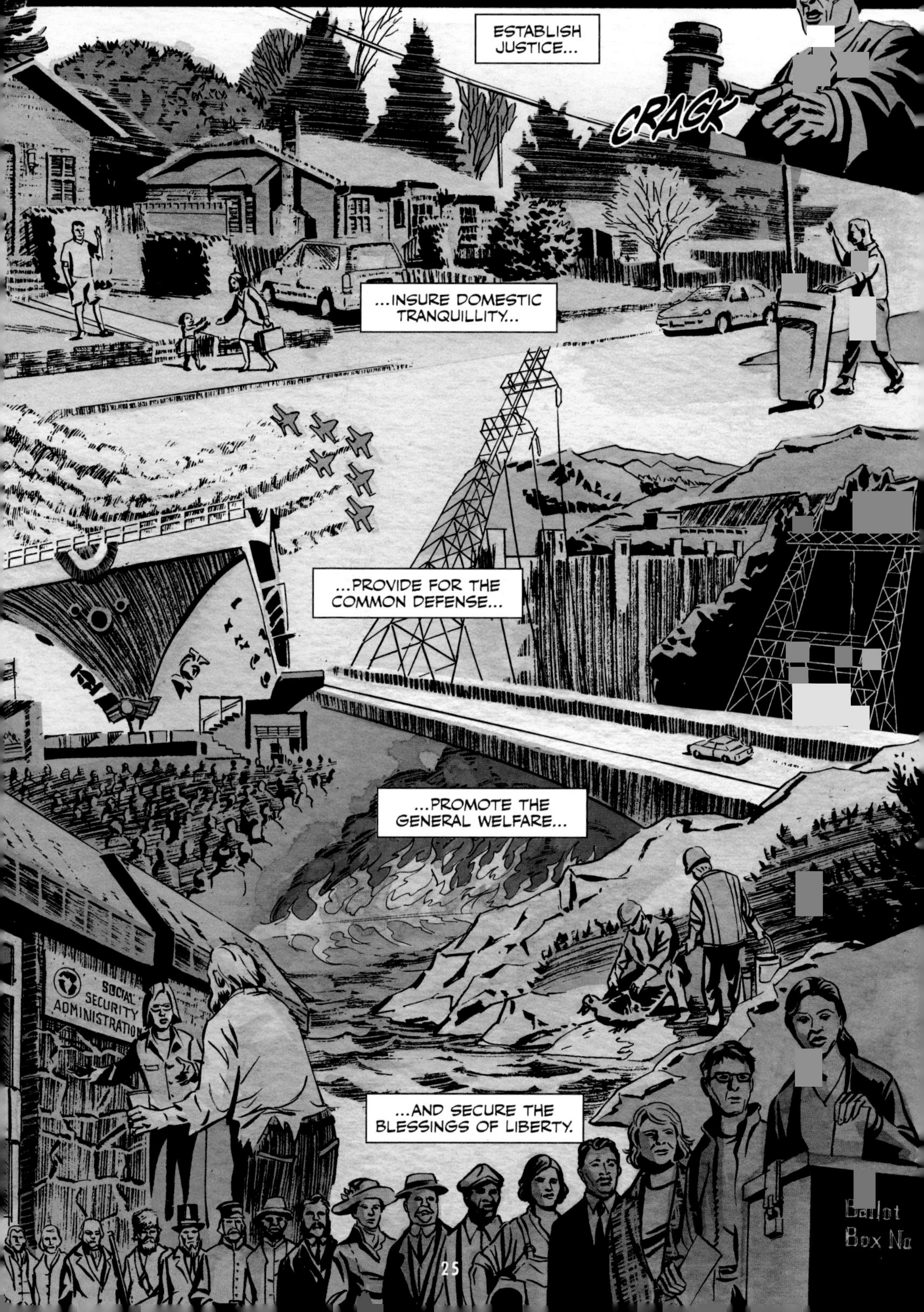

ESTABLISH JUSTICE...
CRACK
...INSURE DOMESTIC TRANQUILLITY...
...PROVIDE FOR THE COMMON DEFENSE...
...PROMOTE THE GENERAL WELFARE...
SOCIAL SECURITY ADMINISTRATION
...AND SECURE THE BLESSINGS OF LIBERTY.
Ballot Box No

THE FIRST SEVEN *ARTICLES* OF THE CONSTITUTION—AS IT WAS COMPOSED IN 1787—OFTEN REFLECT A WILDLY DIFFERENT MORAL UNIVERSE...

...THAN THE ONE WE LIVE IN TODAY.

AT THE TIME, THE VERY IDEA OF "WE THE PEOPLE" APPLIED ONLY TO WHITE MEN—AND OFTEN *EXCLUSIVELY TO THOSE RICH ENOUGH TO OWN LAND.*

ONLY MEMBERS OF THAT GROUP COULD VOTE OR BE ELECTED TO OFFICE.

MANY LATER CHANGES, OR *AMENDMENTS* TO THE DOCUMENT, HAVE RENDERED SEVERAL PARTS OF THE 1787 CONSTITUTION *OBSOLETE.*

WITH THESE AMENDMENTS, THE CONSTITUTION TODAY FOLLOWS MORE CLOSELY THE MODERN VALUES MOST AMERICANS SHARE.

STILL, TO KNOW THE LEGACY OF POLITICAL EXCLUSION THAT ONCE EXISTED IN THE CONSTITUTION IS TO HAVE A GREATER INSIGHT ON THE MOST UNFLATTERING CHAPTERS OF THE NATION'S HISTORY.

Article 1

ARTICLE I OF THE CONSTITUTION ESTABLISHES THE POWERS AND RESPONSIBILITIES OF THE FIRST BRANCH OF GOVERNMENT...

...THE **LEGISLATIVE BRANCH**...

...ALSO KNOWN AS THE **CONGRESS.**

CONGRESS IS THE BODY OF OFFICIALS WE GIVE THE DUTY OF **LEGISLATING,** OF WRITING THE LAWS...

...OR, IN OTHER WORDS, OF TRANSFORMING THE WILL OF THE PEOPLE INTO **PUBLIC POLICY**—GOALS THAT GOVERNMENT DECIDES TO PURSUE.

THAT THE FRAMERS SAW CONGRESS AS THE MOST IMPORTANT BRANCH OF GOVERNMENT IS CLEAR TO SEE. ARTICLE I IS THE FIRST AND LONGEST PART OF THE CONSTITUTION.

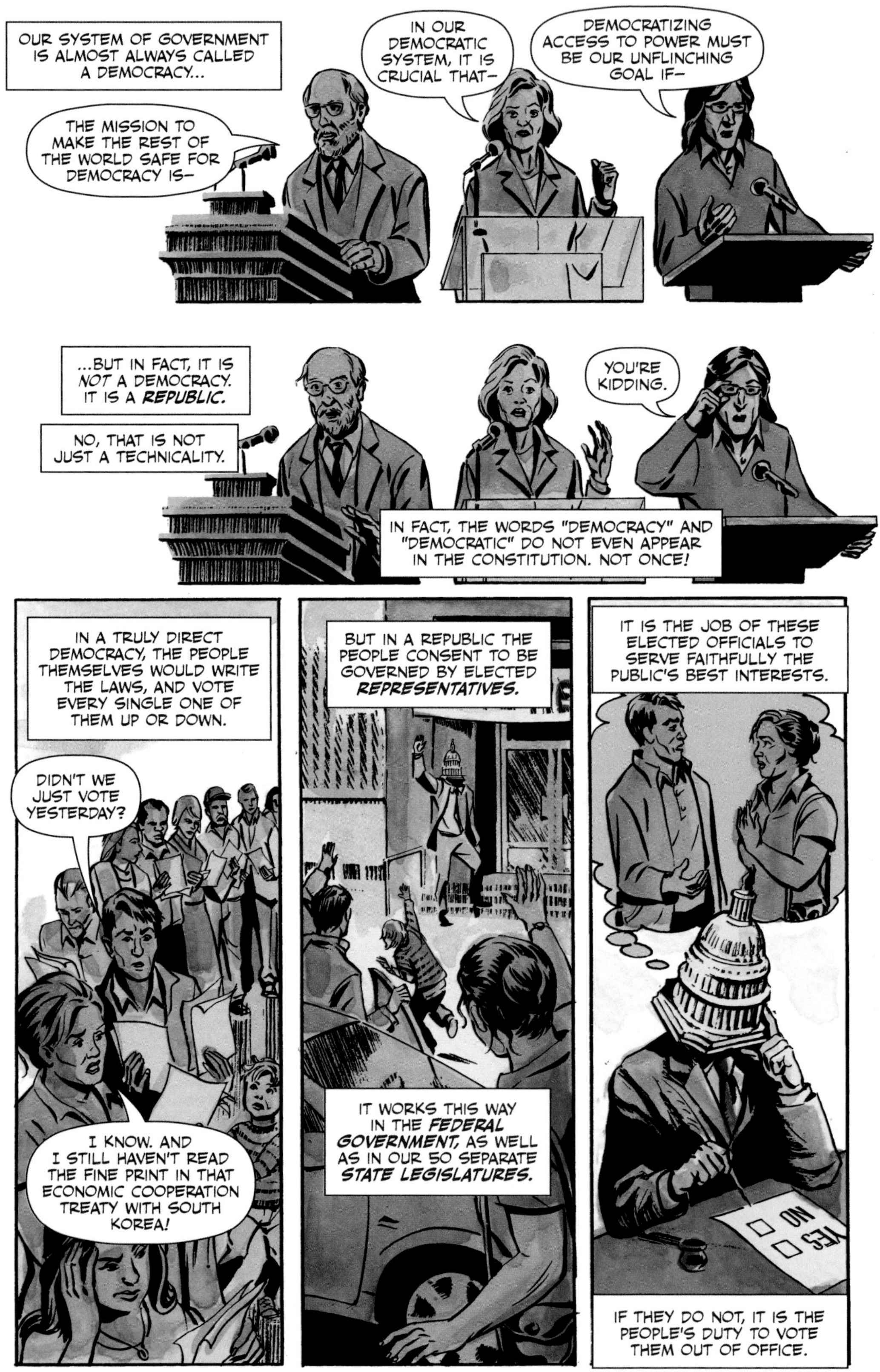
OUR SYSTEM OF GOVERNMENT IS ALMOST ALWAYS CALLED A DEMOCRACY...
THE MISSION TO MAKE THE REST OF THE WORLD SAFE FOR DEMOCRACY IS–
IN OUR DEMOCRATIC SYSTEM, IT IS CRUCIAL THAT–
DEMOCRATIZING ACCESS TO POWER MUST BE OUR UNFLINCHING GOAL IF–
...BUT IN FACT, IT IS *NOT* A DEMOCRACY. IT IS A ***REPUBLIC.***
NO, THAT IS NOT JUST A TECHNICALITY.
YOU'RE KIDDING.
IN FACT, THE WORDS "DEMOCRACY" AND "DEMOCRATIC" DO NOT EVEN APPEAR IN THE CONSTITUTION. NOT ONCE!
IN A TRULY DIRECT DEMOCRACY, THE PEOPLE THEMSELVES WOULD WRITE THE LAWS, AND VOTE EVERY SINGLE ONE OF THEM UP OR DOWN.
DIDN'T WE JUST VOTE YESTERDAY?
I KNOW. AND I STILL HAVEN'T READ THE FINE PRINT IN THAT ECONOMIC COOPERATION TREATY WITH SOUTH KOREA!
BUT IN A REPUBLIC THE PEOPLE CONSENT TO BE GOVERNED BY ELECTED ***REPRESENTATIVES.***
IT WORKS THIS WAY IN THE ***FEDERAL GOVERNMENT,*** AS WELL AS IN OUR 50 SEPARATE ***STATE LEGISLATURES.***
IT IS THE JOB OF THESE ELECTED OFFICIALS TO SERVE FAITHFULLY THE PUBLIC'S BEST INTERESTS.
YES
NO
IF THEY DO NOT, IT IS THE PEOPLE'S DUTY TO VOTE THEM OUT OF OFFICE.

THE CONSTITUTION PROVIDES FOR TWO KINDS OF LAWMAKERS IN CONGRESS: *SENATORS* AND MEMBERS OF THE *HOUSE OF REPRESENTATIVES.**

THAT'S WHAT IT MEANS TO HAVE A *BICAMERAL SYSTEM:* TO HAVE TWO *CHAMBERS OF CONGRESS.*

*OFTEN JUST CALLED *"CONGRESSPERSONS"* FOR SHORT.

"BICAMERAL" HAS NOTHING TO DO WITH POLITICAL PARTIES. POLITICAL PARTIES, LIKE REPUBLICANS AND DEMOCRATS, WERE A LATER INVENTION—NOT SET UP BY THE CONSTITUTION.

IN FACT, MANY OF THE FRAMERS DID NOT APPROVE OF POLITICAL PARTIES.

SO, WHY THE BICAMERAL SYSTEM?

AS TO THE RIGHTS OF SUFFRAGE IN THE NATIONAL LEGISLATURE, IT OUGHT TO BE PROPORTIONED TO THE NUMBER OF FREE INHABITANTS.

NO, NO, NO.

THE STATES HAVE A RIGHT TO AN EQUALITY OF REPRESENTATION. THEY ALREADY POSSESS THIS PRIVILEGE IN THE ARTICLES OF CONFEDERATION!

IT WAS THE RESULT OF THE *GREAT COMPROMISE,* THE ONLY WAY THE FRAMERS COULD BREAK A DEADLOCK BETWEEN LARGE AND SMALL STATES.

UNDER THE ARTICLES OF CONFEDERATION, THE STATES WERE ALREADY LIKE SEPARATE COUNTRIES. GETTING THEM TO GIVE UP THAT KIND OF INDEPENDENCE WOULD BE A DOGFIGHT!

IT WAS ASSUMED THAT EVERY STATE WOULD SEEK AS MUCH POWER AS IT POSSIBLY COULD UNDER A NEW FEDERAL GOVERNMENT...

...ESPECIALLY THOSE STATES WITH SMALLER POPULATIONS.

THE SOLUTION: BALANCE POWER SO NO STATE HAD TOO MUCH.

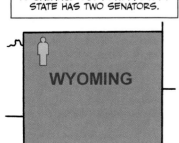

TO BALANCE OUT POWER, EVERY STATE HAS TWO SENATORS.

WYOMING

CALIFORNIA

SO AS FAR AS THINGS IN THE SENATE GO, TODAY'S WYOMING, WITH JUST OVER 500,000 RESIDENTS, HAS THE SAME AMOUNT OF INFLUENCE OVER WHAT HAPPENS IN AMERICA AS CALIFORNIA...

...WITH OVER *33 MILLION.*

29

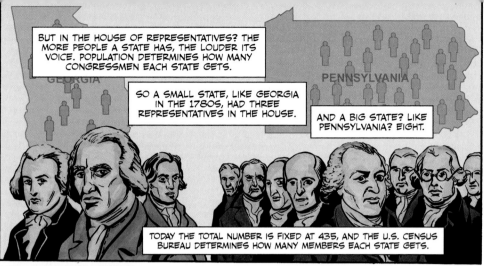

BUT IN THE HOUSE OF REPRESENTATIVES? THE MORE PEOPLE A STATE HAS, THE LOUDER ITS VOICE. POPULATION DETERMINES HOW MANY CONGRESSMEN EACH STATE GETS.

GEORGIA

PENNSYLVANIA

SO A SMALL STATE, LIKE GEORGIA IN THE 1780S, HAD THREE REPRESENTATIVES IN THE HOUSE.

AND A BIG STATE? LIKE PENNSYLVANIA? EIGHT.

TODAY THE TOTAL NUMBER IS FIXED AT 435, AND THE U.S. CENSUS BUREAU DETERMINES HOW MANY MEMBERS EACH STATE GETS.

BUT PROPORTIONAL REPRESENTATION WAS ANOTHER POLITICAL MINEFIELD FOR THE FRAMERS.

SHOULD EVERY INHABITANT COUNT? OR JUST SOME?

FREE WOMEN, WHO WOULD NOT BE ALLOWED TO VOTE FOR ANOTHER 131 YEARS, WERE COUNTED...

...BUT NATIVE AMERICANS WERE NOT.

SOUTHERN STATES WANTED THEIR AFRICAN-AMERICAN SLAVES COUNTED TOO, EVEN THOUGH SLAVES COULD NOT VOTE.

REMEMBER, THE MORE PEOPLE, THE MORE POWER.

AT THE CONSTITUTION'S WRITING, SLAVERY WAS LEGAL IN ALL 13 STATES. BUT IN 1788, 90% OF ALL SLAVES WERE IN THE SOUTH. AND THE MAJORITY OF AMERICANS LOOKING TO END HUMAN BONDAGE WERE IN THE NORTH.

FOR THIS, AND OTHER REASONS, NORTHERNERS WANTED TO KEEP SLAVES FROM BEING COUNTED.

IT WAS PENNSYLVANIA'S JAMES WILSON WHO SUGGESTED THE *THREE-FIFTHS COMPROMISE.*

REFERRING TO SLAVES IN POLITE CODE AS "OTHER PERSONS," THE CONSTITUTION ORIGINALLY DECREED THAT EACH SLAVE WOULD BE COUNTED AS THREE-FIFTHS— OR 60%—OF A FREE MAN OR WOMAN.

TODAY THIS SEEMS REPUGNANT TO THE IDEAS OF LIBERTY THAT FOUNDED THE NATION...

...BUT AT THE TIME NO ONE SAW ANY OTHER WAY TO UNITE THE STATES INTO ONE COUNTRY.

DON'T FORGET, A HORRIFIC *CIVIL WAR* WAS TO BE FOUGHT OVER THIS ISSUE 74 YEARS LATER.

THE THREE-FIFTHS COMPROMISE WOUND UP EMPOWERING SLAVE MASTERS AND THE STATES THEY OFTEN GOVERNED.

EVEN WITH THE THREE-FIFTHS "DISCOUNT," AS THE SLAVE POPULATION GREW, THE SOUTH BECAME MORE AND MORE POLITICALLY POWERFUL.

VIRGINIA CAME UP THE BIG WINNER. FOR 32 OUT OF THE FIRST 36 YEARS OF THE COUNTRY, THE PRESIDENTS WERE ALL SLAVE-OWNING VIRGINIANS.

GEORGE WASHINGTON: 1789–1797.

THOMAS JEFFERSON: 1801–1809.

JAMES MADISON: 1809–1817.

JAMES MONROE: 1817–1825.

THE HOUSE OF REPRESENTATIVES IS THE CHAMBER MOST INTENDED TO REPRESENT "THE PEOPLE."

CONGRESSPERSONS ARE ELECTED EVERY TWO YEARS. IN THIS WAY, THE PEOPLE THEY REPRESENT—THEIR *CONSTITUENTS*—CAN MORE EASILY VOTE THEM IN OR OUT.

ON THE SUBJECT OF VOTING...

...WHEN THE CONSTITUTION WAS FIRST WRITTEN, VOTING RIGHTS, OR *SUFFRAGE*—THE RULES COVERING JUST WHO GETS TO VOTE—WERE DETERMINED BY THE STATES. SOMEONE WITH THE RIGHT TO VOTE IN NORTH CAROLINA MIGHT NOT HAVE THE RIGHT TO VOTE IN MARYLAND.

LAWS HAVE SINCE ALTERED THIS, BUT REMEMBER THAT BACK THEN THE VOTE WAS GIVEN EXCLUSIVELY TO WHITE MEN— AND OFTEN ONLY THOSE WHO OWNED LAND.

RHODE ISLAND WAS THE LAST STATE TO GET RID OF THE LANDOWNING RESTRICTION, IN 1888.

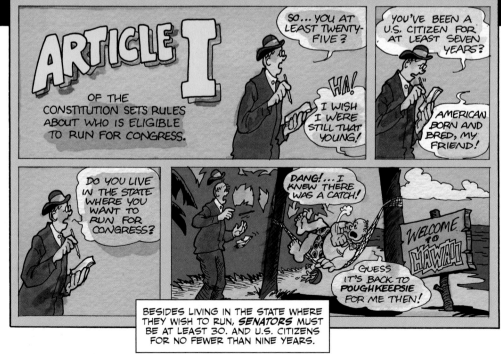

ARTICLE I

OF THE CONSTITUTION SETS RULES ABOUT WHO IS ELIGIBLE TO RUN FOR CONGRESS.

SO... YOU AT LEAST TWENTY-FIVE?

HA! I WISH I WERE STILL THAT YOUNG!

YOU'VE BEEN A U.S. CITIZEN FOR AT LEAST SEVEN YEARS?

AMERICAN BORN AND BRED, MY FRIEND!

DO YOU LIVE IN THE STATE WHERE YOU WANT TO RUN FOR CONGRESS?

DANG!... I KNEW THERE WAS A CATCH!

GUESS IT'S BACK TO *POUGHKEEPSIE* FOR ME THEN!

WELCOME TO HAWAII

BESIDES LIVING IN THE STATE WHERE THEY WISH TO RUN, *SENATORS* MUST BE AT LEAST 30. AND U.S. CITIZENS FOR NO FEWER THAN NINE YEARS.

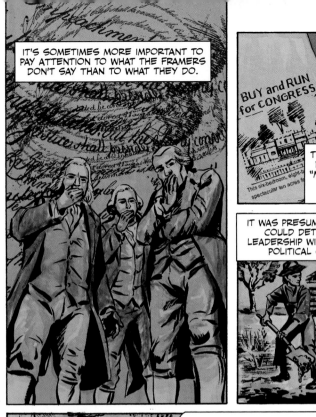

IT'S SOMETIMES MORE IMPORTANT TO PAY ATTENTION TO WHAT THE FRAMERS DON'T SAY THAN TO WHAT THEY DO.

EVEN THOUGH IN THE 1780s MOST FREE WHITE MEN NEEDED TO OWN LAND TO VOTE...

BUY and RUN for CONGRESS

...THE CONSTITUTION HAS NO SIMILAR RULE ABOUT OWNING PROPERTY OR BEING RICH TO BECOME A LEADER IN *ANY* BRANCH OF GOVERNMENT.

THE FRAMERS WANTED THE DOOR TO PUBLIC OFFICE OPEN TO PEOPLE OF "MERIT OF EVERY DESCRIPTION." THIS WAS A RADICALLY PROGRESSIVE APPROACH, FOR THE TIME.

IT WAS PRESUMED THE PROPERTIED VOTING CLASS COULD DETERMINE MERIT, ENSURING GOOD LEADERSHIP WITHOUT ENCOURAGING A HEREDITARY POLITICAL CLASS—AS EXISTED IN EUROPE.

THANKS TO THIS, SOME OF THE NATION'S MOST INFLUENTIAL LEADERS CAME FROM MODEST BEGINNINGS.

EXTRA, EXTRA! CONGRESSMAN RESIGNS IN SHAME!

WHEN A MEMBER OF CONGRESS DIES, RESIGNS, OR IS EXPELLED FROM OFFICE BY A 2/3 MAJORITY VOTE OF EITHER THE HOUSE OR SENATE...

...THE GOVERNOR OF THAT STATE CALLS A SPECIAL ELECTION* TO REPLACE HIM OR HER.

*EXCEPT WHERE STATE LAW ALLOWS A NEW SENATOR TO BE SIMPLY APPOINTED.

SENATORS REPRESENT THEIR STATES' ENTIRE POPULATIONS...

...WHILE MEMBERS OF CONGRESS—AT LEAST THOSE FROM MORE POPULOUS STATES—REPRESENT *DISTRICTS*. THIS PUTS THEM ON A MORE FAMILIAR FOOTING WITH THE PEOPLE AND ISSUES OF A PARTICULAR REGION.

THE IDEA OF DISTRICTS IS NOT DIRECTLY FROM THE CONSTITUTION, BUT THE USE OF DISTRICTS HELPS KEEP ONE POLITICAL PARTY FROM DOMINATING A STATE'S ENTIRE CONGRESSIONAL DELEGATION.

WASHINGTON STATE

WASHINGTON STATE
Congressional

THE SENATE, THE "HIGHER" CHAMBER OF CONGRESS, WAS ORIGINALLY MEANT TO REPRESENT NOT THE PEOPLE BUT THE STATES.

IN FACT, THE CONSTITUTION ORIGINALLY EXCLUDED "WE, THE PEOPLE" FROM VOTING FOR SENATORS! UNTIL 1913 THEY WERE ELECTED BY MEMBERS OF STATE LEGISLATURES.

SENATORS SERVE FOR SIX-YEAR *TERMS IN OFFICE.*

IT'S POSSIBLE FOR ALL MEMBERS OF THE HOUSE TO BE VOTED OUT OF OFFICE EVERY TWO YEARS. BUT IN THE SENATE...

...ELECTIONS ARE STAGGERED SO ALL SENATORS NEVER COME UP FOR REELECTION AT THE SAME TIME.

THIS TENDS TO MAKE THE SENATE MORE STABLE AND LESS REACTIVE TO SUDDEN CHANGES IN THE MOOD OF THE COUNTRY.

ARTICLE I GRANTS BOTH CHAMBERS OF CONGRESS THE AUTHORITY TO MAKE THEIR OWN RULES AND PICK THEIR OWN OFFICERS.

THIS MEANS PRACTICES LIKE FORMING COMMITTEES, FILIBUSTERS, AND POINTS OF ORDER AND OFFICES LIKE MINORITY AND MAJORITY LEADERS AND WHIPS ARE NOT DIRECTLY FROM THE CONSTITUTION.

THE VICE PRESIDENT SERVES AS PRESIDENT OF THE SENATE. BUT HE GETS TO CAST A VOTE ONLY IN THE EVENT OF A TIE.

VICE PRESIDENT *CHESTER A. ARTHUR,* 1881, BREAKING A TIE VOTE.

GEORGE WASHINGTON'S VICE PRESIDENT, *JOHN ADAMS,* HOLDS THE RECORD WITH 26 TIE-BREAKING VOTES. (WITH JUST 13 STATES THEN, THERE WERE ONLY 26 SENATORS—UNLIKE THE 100 WE HAVE NOW.)

TO PRESIDE IN THE VICE PRESIDENT'S ABSENCE, THE SENATE ELECTS A *PRESIDENT PRO TEMPORE,* BY MODERN TRADITION THE MOST SENIOR MEMBER OF THE PARTY THAT HOLDS THE MOST SEATS.

WHAT IF A HIGH-RANKING FEDERAL OFFICIAL IS ACCUSED OF A SERIOUS BREACH OF THE PUBLIC TRUST?

THE CONSTITUTION GIVES THE HOUSE THE POWER TO *IMPEACH*—MEANING "BRING CHARGES AGAINST"—THE PRESIDENT, VICE PRESIDENT, CABINET MEMBERS, AND SUPREME COURT AND FEDERAL JUDGES. CHARGES CAN BE FOR TREASON, BRIBERY, OR OTHER "HIGH CRIMES AND MISDEMEANORS"...

...ALTHOUGH WHAT EXACTLY THAT ENTAILS IS OFTEN A MATTER OF DEBATE...

PRESIDENT ANDREW JOHNSON, IMPEACHED BY CONGRESS, 1868.

PRESIDENT WILLIAM JEFFERSON CLINTON, IMPEACHED BY CONGRESS, 1998.

SECRETARY OF WAR WILLIAM BELKNAP, IMPEACHED BY CONGRESS, 1876.

FEDERAL JUDGE ALCEE HASTINGS, IMPEACHED BY CONGRESS, 1988.

$!@$!^*#%!%!

IN IMPEACHMENT CASES, THE SENATE ACTS AS THE JURY, INVESTIGATING THE CHARGES AND THEN VOTING TO *CONVICT* OR *ACQUIT*.

ONLY SEVEN PEOPLE—ALL JUDGES—HAVE ACTUALLY BEEN CONVICTED BY THE SENATE, WHICH MUST THEN EXERCISE ITS POWER TO REMOVE PEOPLE FROM OFFICE.

BUT IT CANNOT SEND THEM TO JAIL.

JUDGE JOHN PICKERING WAS THE FIRST MAN TO BE CONVICTED IN AN IMPEACHMENT PROCEEDING. HE WAS REMOVED FROM OFFICE IN 1804. HIS CRIME? DRUNKENNESS ON THE JOB.

IT IS UP TO THE STATES TO CONDUCT ELECTIONS...

ALTHOUGH AN 1848 LAW CREATED A UNIFORM *ELECTION DAY* ON THE FIRST TUESDAY AFTER THE FIRST MONDAY IN NOVEMBER.

...BUT CONGRESS HAS THE POWER TO TAKE ACTION IF THE ELECTIONS ARE INEFFICIENT, UNFAIR, OR TAINTED BY BRIBERY OR FRAUD.

BALLOT BOX

AT FIRST THE CONSTITUTION STIPULATED THAT CONGRESS MEET AT LEAST ONCE A YEAR AND APPOINTED THE CONGRESSIONAL SESSION TO BEGIN, IN MOST CASES, MORE THAN A YEAR AFTER THE ELECTION.

MAY

QUACK!

QUACK! QUACK!

QUACK!

IN 1933 THE CONSTITUTION WAS CHANGED, SETTING NEW, FIRM DATES FOR TERMS IN OFFICE TO END.

QUACK!

QUACK!

SHOO!

QUACK!

THIS GAVE *LAME DUCKS*— POLITICIANS WHO HAVE LOST THEIR MOST RECENT ELECTION BUT ARE STILL SERVING THEIR TERMS—LOTS OF REMAINING TIME IN OFFICE.

WHEN IT COMES TO CONGRESS, THE FRAMERS WERE SPECIFIC ABOUT A FEW MORE THINGS.

TO PREVENT SMALL NUMBERS OF LAWMAKERS FROM HIJACKING CONGRESS'S POWER...

RING

...MORE THAN HALF THE MEMBERS OF EITHER CHAMBER MUST BE PRESENT TO CONDUCT OFFICIAL BUSINESS. THIS IS CALLED A *QUORUM*.

RING

RING

BELLS AND LIGHTS LIKE THESE ARE MOUNTED THROUGHOUT THE CAPITOL COMPLEX TO SUMMON CONGRESSMEN TO QUORUM CALLS.

EVEN A SUBWAY SYSTEM WAS DEVELOPED AT THE CAPITOL FOR TRANSPORTING LEGISLATORS FROM THEIR OFFICES TO THEIR CHAMBERS.

CONGRESS MUST ALSO KEEP JOURNALS OF ITS PROCEEDINGS AND VOTES...

...AND, BY PUBLISHING THEM, MAKE THEM ACCESSIBLE TO THE PUBLIC.

THE HOUSE AND SENATE MUST FUNCTION TOGETHER TO GET LAWS PASSED. SO THERE ARE RULES TO KEEP THEM IN SESSION AT THE SAME TIME.

THE SENATE WILL COME TO ORDER...

RAP RAP RAP

FOR EXAMPLE, UNLESS ONE CHAMBER GETS THE PERMISSION OF THE OTHER, EACH IS OBLIGATED TO MEET AT LEAST ONCE EVERY FOUR DAYS...

...EVEN IF IT'S JUST FOR A FEW SECONDS.

...AND HEREBY ADJOURN FOR THE DAY!

RAP RAP

BRIEF MEETINGS LIKE THIS ARE CALLED *PRO FORMA* SESSIONS.

HISTORICALLY, IN EUROPE KINGS AND QUEENS COULD SIMPLY TAKE LEGISLATORS WHOSE VIEWS THEY DIDN'T AGREE WITH AND JAIL THEM AT WILL.

I HAVE COME TO ARREST THE TRAITORS PYM, HAMPDEN, HOLLES, HESILRIGE, AND STRODE!

TO KEEP MEMBERS OF CONGRESS FROM BEING BULLIED BY POLITICAL ENEMIES...

STOP THE DEBATE! STOP OR I'LL SUE!

I'LL SUE!

SUMMONS

...ARTICLE I, SECTION 6 SHIELDS THEM FROM ARREST AND FROM LAWSUITS WHILE CARRYING OUT THEIR DUTIES...

UMPF!

SLAM!

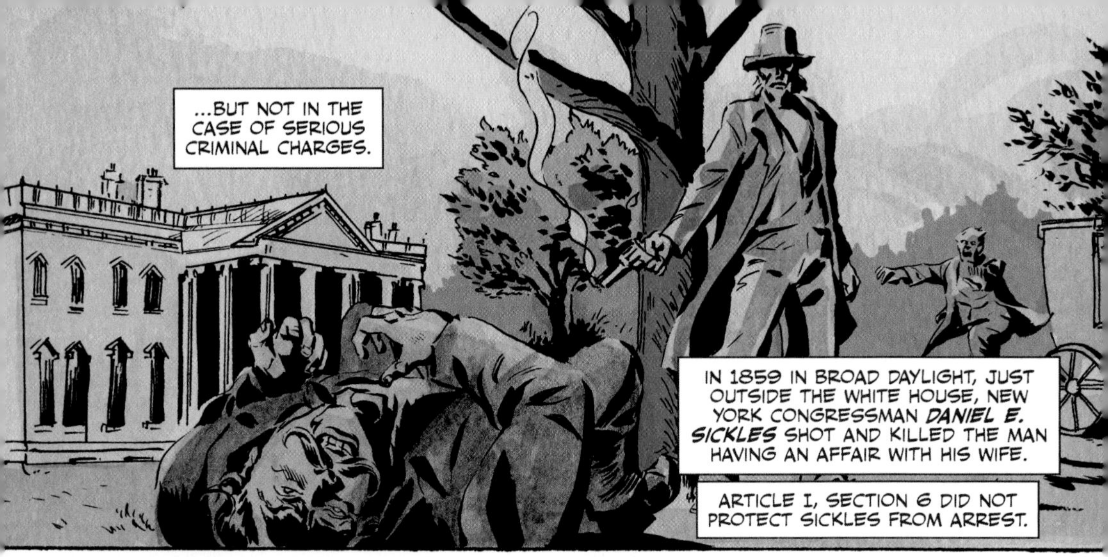
...BUT NOT IN THE CASE OF SERIOUS CRIMINAL CHARGES.
IN 1859 IN BROAD DAYLIGHT, JUST OUTSIDE THE WHITE HOUSE, NEW YORK CONGRESSMAN ***DANIEL E. SICKLES*** SHOT AND KILLED THE MAN HAVING AN AFFAIR WITH HIS WIFE.
ARTICLE I, SECTION 6 DID NOT PROTECT SICKLES FROM ARREST.

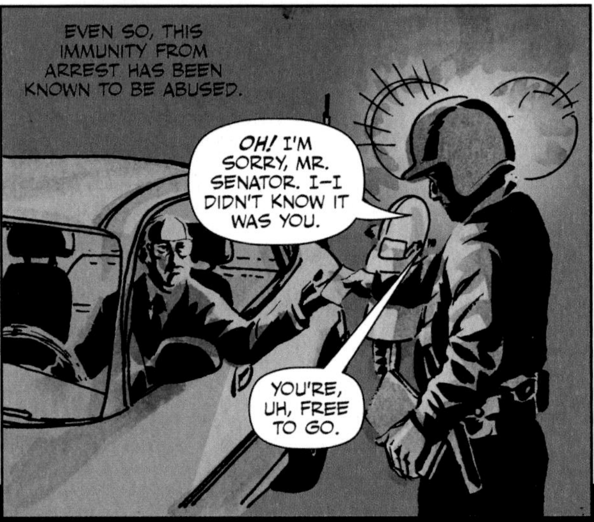
EVEN SO, THIS IMMUNITY FROM ARREST HAS BEEN KNOWN TO BE ABUSED.
OH! I'M SORRY, MR. SENATOR. I—I DIDN'T KNOW IT WAS YOU.
YOU'RE, UH, FREE TO GO.

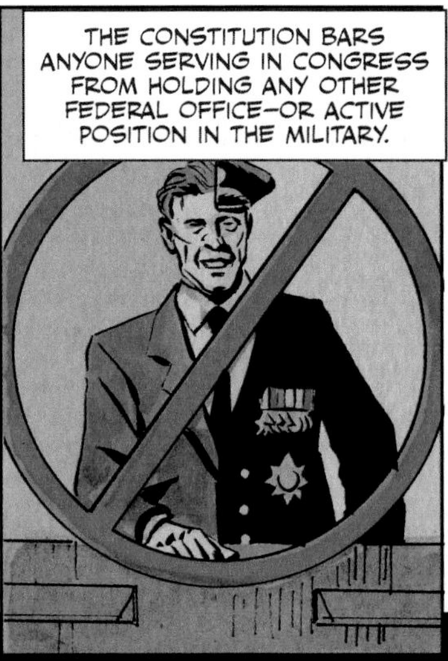
THE CONSTITUTION BARS ANYONE SERVING IN CONGRESS FROM HOLDING ANY OTHER FEDERAL OFFICE—OR ACTIVE POSITION IN THE MILITARY.

TO CARRY OUT ANY OF ITS OPERATIONS, NOT THE LEAST OF WHICH IS SECURING THE COUNTRY AGAINST FOREIGN INVADERS AND MAINTAINING THE RULE OF LAW, THE GOVERNMENT NEEDS TO RAISE ***REVENUE.***

HOW DOES IT RAISE MONEY? IN LARGE PART BY COLLECTING ***TAXES.***

TAXES ARE ANOTHER KIND OF LAW, MOST OF WHICH START OUT AS ***BILLS,*** WRITTEN PROPOSALS TO ENACT (OR REPEAL) A LAW.

MOST LAWS CAN BE INTRODUCED IN EITHER CHAMBER OF CONGRESS. BUT, CONSTITUTIONALLY, TAXES MAY ORIGINATE ONLY IN THE HOUSE OF REPRESENTATIVES.

Article. 1. Section. 7. Clause 2:

How a Bill Becomes a Law.

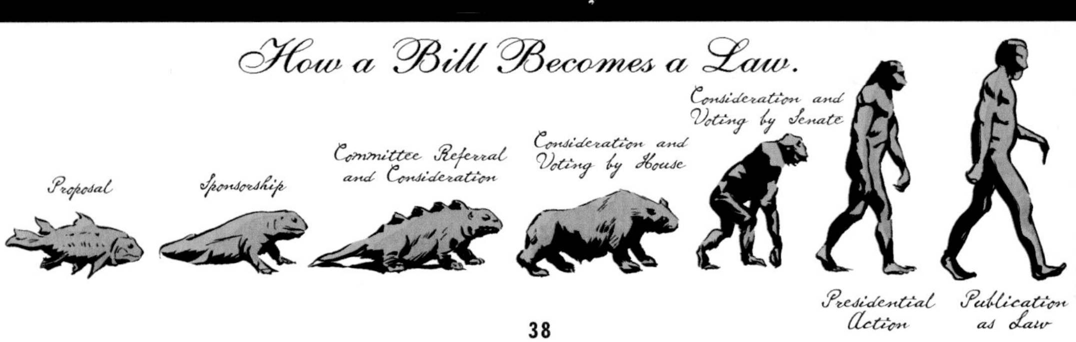
Proposal
Sponsorship
Committee Referral and Consideration
Consideration and Voting by House
Consideration and Voting by Senate
Presidential Action
Publication as Law

PASSING LAWS ISN'T EASY. IT'S NOT SUPPOSED TO BE.

LOOK OUT! IT'S GONNA BLOW!

KA POW

OTHERWISE WE MIGHT GET TOO MANY OF THEM.

SOME PEOPLE WOULD SAY THIS HAS ALREADY HAPPENED.

FSSHH!

THUNK THUNK!

So the Constitution outlines a lengthy process for bills to become laws.

39

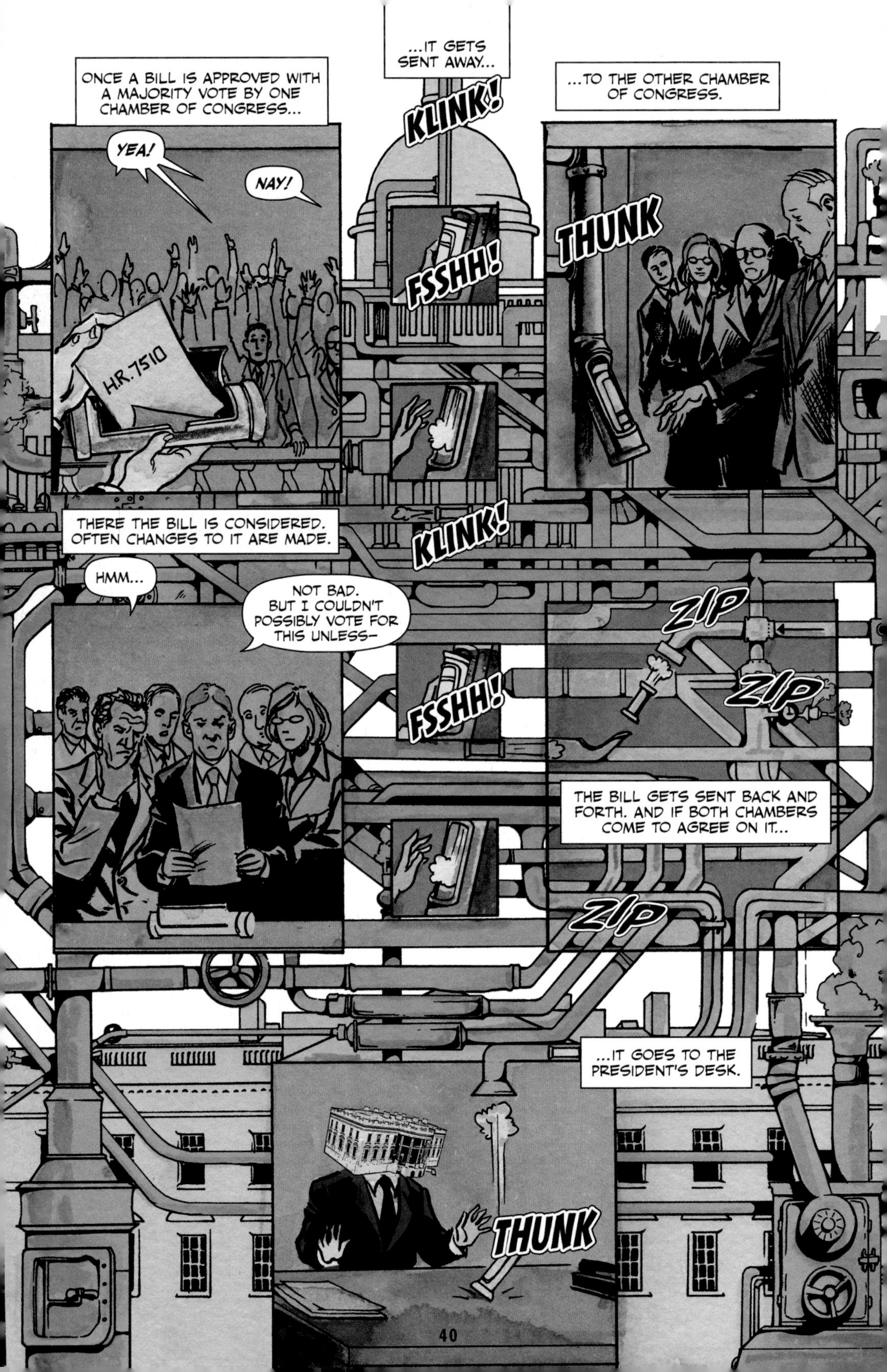
ONCE A BILL IS APPROVED WITH A MAJORITY VOTE BY ONE CHAMBER OF CONGRESS...
YEA!
NAY!
H.R. 7510
...IT GETS SENT AWAY...
KLINK!
FSSHH!
...TO THE OTHER CHAMBER OF CONGRESS.
THUNK
THERE THE BILL IS CONSIDERED. OFTEN CHANGES TO IT ARE MADE.
KLINK!
HMM...
NOT BAD. BUT I COULDN'T POSSIBLY VOTE FOR THIS UNLESS—
FSSHH!
ZIP
ZIP
THE BILL GETS SENT BACK AND FORTH. AND IF BOTH CHAMBERS COME TO AGREE ON IT...
ZIP
...IT GOES TO THE PRESIDENT'S DESK.
THUNK

IF THE PRESIDENT AGREES WITH THE BILL, HE CAN SIGN IT. IT THEN BECOMES LAW.

H.R. 7510

OR THE PRESIDENT CAN DO NOTHING, AND IN TEN DAYS—SUNDAYS NOT COUNTED—THE BILL BECOMES LAW AUTOMATICALLY.*

*UNLESS THE CONGRESSIONAL SESSION ENDS DURING THAT TIME. THEN THE BILL DOES NOT BECOME LAW. THIS IS CALLED A *POCKET VETO.*

BUT IF THE PRESIDENT DOESN'T LIKE THE BILL, HE CAN *VETO* IT.

VETO IS LATIN FOR "I FORBID."

H.R. 7510
VETO

THAT MEANS HE SENDS IT *BACK* TO CONGRESS.

THUNK

—SIGH—

BACK TO THE DRAWING BOARD.

CONGRESS CAN THEN EITHER CHANGE THE BILL AGAIN AND RETURN IT TO THE PRESIDENT, HOPING IT WILL GET PASSED THIS TIME...

...OR *OVERTURN* THE VETO BY VOTING ON THE ORIGINAL BILL AGAIN.

IF THE BILL PASSES IN BOTH CHAMBERS WITH A *SUPERMAJORITY*—A 2/3 VOTE—IT BECOMES LAW REGARDLESS OF THE PRESIDENT'S OPINION.

THIS HAPPENS PRETTY RARELY. BETWEEN 1789 AND 2005, OUT OF 2,550 PRESIDENTIAL VETOES, ONLY 106 WERE OVERTURNED.

PRESIDENT *JOHN TYLER (1841-1845)* WAS THE FIRST PRESIDENT TO HAVE A VETO OVERTURNED. HE WANTED TO BUILD MORE REVENUE CUTTERS, SHIPS IN A SERVICE THAT PREDATED THE MODERN U.S. COAST GUARD. THE BILL HE VETOED DENIED HIM THE AUTHORITY TO SPEND MONEY TO BUILD THE SHIPS WITHOUT CONGRESS'S APPROVAL.

ONLY CONGRESS HAS THE POWER TO RAISE MONEY BY COLLECTING TAXES AND TARIFFS.

EVEN WHEN THE PRESIDENT HAS SOME PROJECT IN MIND, HE MUST ASK CONGRESS FOR FUNDING.

THIS IS ANOTHER EXAMPLE OF CHECKS AND BALANCES.

THE CONSTITUTION ORDERS THAT FEDERAL TAXES MUST BE THE SAME IN EVERY STATE.

36.9¢ FEDERAL GAS TAX

CONGRESS HAS THE POWER TO BORROW MONEY...

7184 3915 5401 8902 U.S CONGRESS VOTES

...WHICH IT OFTEN DOES, FROM BOTH FOREIGN AND DOMESTIC BANKS.

OUR NATIONAL DEBT: $9207920905393.00

YOUR Family Share! $37265.77

IT ALSO IS GIVEN THE AUTHORITY TO "REGULATE COMMERCE" BETWEEN STATES AND WITH FOREIGN COUNTRIES DOING BUSINESS WITH THE UNITED STATES.

Commerce

THIS COMMERCE CLAUSE IS, FAMOUSLY, SOMETHING OF A GRAY AREA IN THE CONSTITUTION. SOME ARGUE THAT BECAUSE ITS LANGUAGE IS SO BROAD, CONGRESS HAS USED IT TO GRAB POWER.

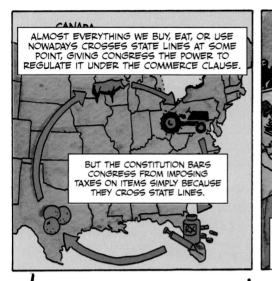

ALMOST EVERYTHING WE BUY, EAT, OR USE NOWADAYS CROSSES STATE LINES AT SOME POINT, GIVING CONGRESS THE POWER TO REGULATE IT UNDER THE COMMERCE CLAUSE.

BUT THE CONSTITUTION BARS CONGRESS FROM IMPOSING TAXES ON ITEMS SIMPLY BECAUSE THEY CROSS STATE LINES.

YOU REALIZE THAT TAKING STEROIDS IS A FEDERAL CRIME, RIGHT? SO DID YOU OR DID YOU NOT KNOW THAT PLAYERS WERE TAKING THEM?

ER... THAT IS TO SAY, I...

CONGRESS HAS EVEN USED THE COMMERCE CLAUSE TO REGULATE PROFESSIONAL BASEBALL.

HOW CITIZENS OF FOREIGN COUNTRIES CAN BECOME U.S. CITIZENS IS CONTROLLED BY CONGRESS...

...AS IS HOW PEOPLE AND BUSINESSES FILE FOR BANKRUPTCY PROTECTION.

ACCOUNT OVERDUE

PRINTING MONEY, PUNISHING COUNTERFEITERS...

...AND RUNNING BOTH THE NATIONAL POST OFFICE...

U.S. MAIL

...AND THE FEDERAL COURT SYSTEM ALL FALL UNDER ARTICLE I'S CONGRESSIONAL AUTHORITY.

CONGRATULATIONS, GUYS.

I THINK YOU FINALLY NAILED IT.

SQUAWK! PIECES OF EIGHT!

HEY! BRING THAT BACK!

TO PROTECT INVENTORS, WRITERS, ARTISTS, AND MUSICIANS FROM HAVING PEOPLE COPY AND EXPLOIT THEIR CREATIVE WORKS...

...CONGRESS ENFORCES PATENTS AND COPYRIGHTS.

IT ALSO FIGHTS ACTUAL PIRACY BY IMPOSING THE RULE OF LAW ON AMERICAN SHIPS ON THE HIGH SEAS AND ALL SHIPS IN AMERICAN TERRITORIAL WATERS.

BOOM

...TO DECLARE WAR...

THE CONSTITUTION GIVES CONGRESS ONE TRULY AWESOME RESPONSIBILITY...

...AND TO ESTABLISH, FUND, AND REGULATE THE MILITARY.

BUT IF YOU WERE ASKED TO NAME THE LAST THREE COUNTRIES CONGRESS ACTUALLY VOTED TO GO TO WAR WITH...

...AND ANSWERED, "IRAQ," "VIETNAM," AND "KOREA," YOU WOULD BE WRONG.

THE CORRECT ANSWER IS ROMANIA, HUNGARY, AND BULGARIA, SIX MONTHS INTO OUR INVOLVEMENT IN WORLD WAR II, IN 1942.

ALTHOUGH EVEN FROM THE BIRTH OF THE COUNTRY, MILITARY FORCE HAS BEEN USED WITHOUT A FORMAL DECLARATION OF WAR...

KOREAN CONFLICT, 1950.

VIETNAM CONFLICT, 1967.

OPERATION DESERT FOX, 1998.

...the Congress approves and supports the determination of the President, as Commander in Chief, to take all necessary measures to repel any armed attack against the forces of the United States and to prevent further aggression...

...IN MODERN TIMES, TROOPS HAVE BEEN REGULARLY SENT INTO ACTION UNDER ORDERS OF THE PRESIDENT, ACTING AS *COMMANDER IN CHIEF,* ALWAYS WITH SOME KIND OF RESOLUTION PASSED BY CONGRESS.

IN A CERTAIN LEGAL SENSE, THEN, THESE CONFLICTS HAVE NOT ACTUALLY BEEN WARS.

IF IT IS NOT SATISFIED WITH THE STATE OF A MILITARY OPERATION, AS WAS THE CASE DURING PRESIDENT RICHARD NIXON'S PROSECUTION OF THE VIETNAM CONFLICT...

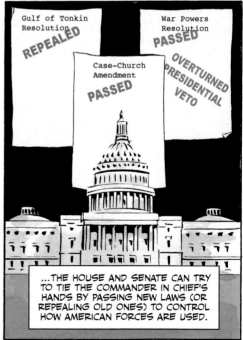

Gulf of Tonkin Resolution

REPEALED

War Powers Resolution

PASSED

Case-Church Amendment

PASSED

OVERTURNED PRESIDENTIAL VETO

...THE HOUSE AND SENATE CAN TRY TO TIE THE COMMANDER IN CHIEF'S HANDS BY PASSING NEW LAWS (OR REPEALING OLD ONES) TO CONTROL HOW AMERICAN FORCES ARE USED.

MORE IMPORTANT, CONGRESS CAN ASSERT ITSELF WITH ITS SO-CALLED *POWER OF THE PURSE.*

!

SNIP

REMEMBER: ONLY *CONGRESS* CAN IMPOSE TAXES, AND APPROVE HOW THE NATION'S MONEY IS SPENT.

BUT AS ANOTHER FORM OF CHECKS AND BALANCES...

the People

...THE CONSTITUTION FORCES CONGRESS TO KEEP TRACK OF THE MONEY IT SPENDS. AND MAKE RECORDS OF ITS ACCOUNTING PUBLIC.

EARLY IN THE NATION'S HISTORY, ALL THE STATES OPERATED *MILITIAS:* FORCES MADE UP OF *CITIZEN VOLUNTEERS* TO DEFEND CITIES AND TOWNS.

TODAY, THE NATIONAL GUARD HAS INHERITED THIS FUNCTION.

ARMY NATIONAL GUARD

ARMY NATIONAL GUARD

AND CONGRESS MAY CALL UP THESE STATE FORCES TO RESPOND TO NATIONAL EMERGENCIES.

ARTICLE I SECTION 8 ALSO CALLS FOR THE ESTABLISHMENT OF A "SEAT OF GOVERNMENT"–WHICH SOON BECAME WASHINGTON, D.C.

CONGRESS RESERVED THE RIGHT TO HAVE FULL JURISDICTION OVER IT.

GEORGE WASHINGTON, CAPTAIN CHARLES L'ENFANT, AND BENJAMIN BANNEKER SURVEYING THE FUTURE SITE OF THE DISTRICT OF COLUMBIA.

THE FRAMERS KNEW THAT IN THE LIMITED AMOUNT OF TIME THEY HAD TO WRITE THE CONSTITUTION, THEY MIGHT NOT HAVE ANTICIPATED EVERY KIND OF POWER CONGRESS WOULD NEED.

...SO THEY INCLUDED WHAT HAS BECOME KNOWN AS...

To make all Laws which shall be necessary, and proper **elastic**

...THE *ELASTIC CLAUSE*, OR...

...THE *BASKET CLAUSE.* IT GIVES CONGRESS THE RIGHT TO MAKE ALL "NECESSARY AND PROPER" LAWS IT NEEDS TO FULFILL ITS FUNCTION.

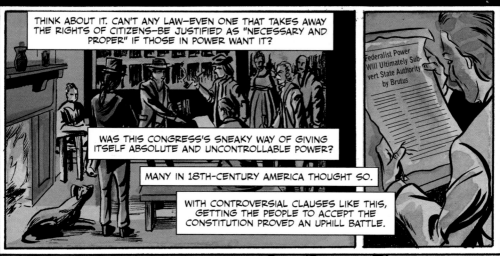

THINK ABOUT IT. CAN'T ANY LAW—EVEN ONE THAT TAKES AWAY THE RIGHTS OF CITIZENS—BE JUSTIFIED AS "NECESSARY AND PROPER" IF THOSE IN POWER WANT IT?

WAS THIS CONGRESS'S SNEAKY WAY OF GIVING ITSELF ABSOLUTE AND UNCONTROLLABLE POWER?

MANY IN 18TH-CENTURY AMERICA THOUGHT SO.

WITH CONTROVERSIAL CLAUSES LIKE THIS, GETTING THE PEOPLE TO ACCEPT THE CONSTITUTION PROVED AN UPHILL BATTLE.

Federalist Power Will Ultimately Subvert State Authority by Brutus

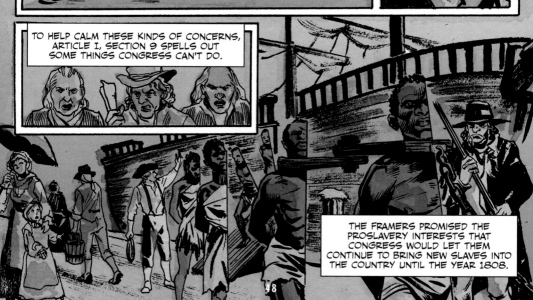

TO HELP CALM THESE KINDS OF CONCERNS, ARTICLE I, SECTION 9 SPELLS OUT SOME THINGS CONGRESS CAN'T DO.

THE FRAMERS PROMISED THE PROSLAVERY INTERESTS THAT CONGRESS WOULD LET THEM CONTINUE TO BRING NEW SLAVES INTO THE COUNTRY UNTIL THE YEAR 1808.

48

Article 1 Section 9, Clause 2: Habeas Corpus

THROUGHOUT MUCH OF HISTORY AND IN MANY COUNTRIES, PEOPLE HAVE BEEN SIMPLY BRANDED "ENEMIES OF THE STATE," ARRESTED...

...AND NEVER HEARD FROM AGAIN.

BUT FREE PEOPLE HAVE THE PRIVILEGE OF *HABEAS CORPUS:* TO APPEAR IN PUBLIC COURT AND CHALLENGE THE LEGITIMACY OF THEIR ARREST AND DETENTION.

IT IS ONE OF THE CORNERSTONE LIBERTIES OF ANY FREE SOCIETY.

HABEAS CORPUS MEANS "HAVE THE BODY"–TO PROVE THAT PRISONERS HAVE NOT BEEN DISAPPEARED. IT DOES NOT MEAN THAT ONE CAN BE CONVICTED OF MURDER ONLY IF THE VICTIM'S REMAINS HAVE BEEN FOUND.

THE CONSTITUTION PROTECTS HABEAS CORPUS BY STATING IT "SHALL NOT BE SUSPENDED"...

...EXCEPT IN TIMES OF INVASION OR REBELLION.

PRESIDENT *ABRAHAM LINCOLN (1861-1865)* FAMOUSLY SUSPENDED HABEAS CORPUS IN MARYLAND DURING THE CIVIL WAR.

HE CLAIMED TO NEED POWER TO ARREST PRO-*CONFEDERATE* AGITATORS IN THAT STATE TO KEEP IT FROM *SECEDING FROM THE UNION.*

IF MARYLAND HAD JOINED THE SOUTH, WASHINGTON, D.C., WOULD HAVE BEEN SURROUNDED AND NEARLY INDEFENSIBLE.

ACTS OF ATTAINDER ALLOWED THE BRITISH PARLIAMENT, THE KING, AND EVEN AMERICAN STATE GOVERNMENTS TO SIMPLY PRONOUNCE PERSONS AND GROUPS GUILTY OF A CRIME WITHOUT A TRIAL AND CONFISCATE THEIR PROPERTIES.

THE CONSTITUTION BANS BOTH THE FEDERAL AND STATE GOVERNMENTS FROM THIS PRACTICE...

...AS IT DOES EX POST FACTO* LAWS.

SAY THAT WHILE DRIVING, YOU TAKE A RIGHT TURN AT A RED LIGHT...

...AND THE NEXT DAY A NEW LAW MAKING THAT KIND OF TURN ILLEGAL GOES INTO EFFECT.

*LATIN FOR "AFTER THE FACT."

UNDER THE CONSTITUTION, NO EX POST FACTO LAW CAN TURN AN ACT INTO A CRIME BEFORE THAT LAW IS ACTUALLY ON THE BOOKS.

TRAFFIC VIOLATION

PAY THIS AMOUNT: $240.00

ARTICLE I ORIGINALLY STOPPED CONGRESS FROM COLLECTING *PROPERTY* OR *INCOME TAXES*...

...BUT IN 1913 CONGRESS WAS GIVEN THAT POWER BY THE 16TH AMENDMENT.

THE FEDERAL GOVERNMENT *CANNOT* IMPOSE TAXES ON ITEMS THAT CROSS STATE LINES...

...BUT IT *CAN* IMPOSE SPECIAL CHARGES CALLED *DUTIES* OR *TARIFFS* ON GOODS THAT ARRIVE FROM FOREIGN COUNTRIES.

ONE FINAL POWER DENIED TO CONGRESS UNDER ARTICLE I WAS AN UNAMBIGUOUS LEAP FORWARD FOR EQUALITY.

IT ALSO STRUCK A BLOW AGAINST EUROPE'S HEREDITARY NOBILITY.

EVEN AT THE TIME OF THE AMERICAN REVOLUTION, EVERYDAY CITIZENS PAID TRIBUTE WHEN PASSING "GENTLEMEN" IN THE STREET.

BACK THEN IT WAS WIDELY THOUGHT THAT THE BROAD MASS OF THE PEOPLE WAS NOT SOPHISTICATED ENOUGH TO UNDERSTAND POLITICS.

SO WHEN CLAUSE 8 AFFIRMS THAT "NO TITLE OF NOBILITY SHALL BE GRANTED BY THE UNITED STATES"...

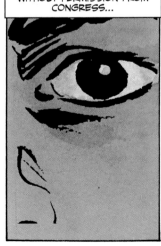

...AND THAT NO GOVERNMENT OFFICERS MAY RECEIVE SUCH TITLES FROM FOREIGN STATES WITHOUT PERMISSION FROM CONGRESS...

...IT STRIKES A BLOW FOR DEMOCRATIC IDEALS, ONE THAT IT FAILED TO DO ON ISSUES LIKE SLAVERY.

YET THE CONCEPT OF ABOLISHING ROYALTY WAS GENUINELY A REVOLUTION.

MY MOCKINGBIRD CAN BEAT YOUR WILLOW GOLDFINCH TO A PULP!

OH, YEAH?

PROVE IT!

GENERALLY, BEFORE THE 1900s AMERICANS IDENTIFIED WITH THEIR STATES MORE THAN WITH THE NATION.

SINCE THE STATES HAD BEEN TOO POWERFUL UNDER THE ARTICLES OF CONFEDERATION, AND THE CENTRAL GOVERNMENT TOO WEAK, THE FRAMERS USED ARTICLE I TO RESTRICT WHAT STATES CAN AND CAN'T DO.

SO THE CONSTITUTION BANS THE STATES FROM PRINTING THEIR OWN MONEY...

...AND FROM KEEPING THEIR OWN MILITARIES IN TIMES OF PEACE...

...AND FROM MAKING TREATIES WITH FOREIGN GOVERNMENTS...

Oklahoma-New Zealand Alliance

...AT LEAST NOT WITHOUT THE PERMISSION OF 2/3 OF BOTH CHAMBERS OF CONGRESS.

Article. II.

ARTICLE II OF THE CONSTITUTION ESTABLISHES THE POWERS AND RESPONSIBILITIES OF THE SECOND BRANCH OF GOVERNMENT...

...THE **EXECUTIVE.**

THE EXECUTIVE BRANCH IS LED BY THE **PRESIDENT,** WHO BY LAW MUST BE A NATURAL-BORN CITIZEN* AND AT LEAST 35 YEARS OF AGE, AND HAVE BEEN RESIDING IN THE UNITED STATES FOR AT LEAST 14 YEARS.

THE EXECUTIVE BRANCH ALSO INCLUDES THE PRESIDENT'S **CABINET,** WHICH CONSISTS OF THE **VICE PRESIDENT** AND THE HEADS OF THE (CURRENTLY) 15 **EXECUTIVE DEPARTMENTS.**

TOGETHER THEIR DUTY IS TO PUT INTO PRACTICE—TO EXECUTE AND ENFORCE— THE LAWS THAT CONGRESS PASSES.

IT'S WORTH REPEATING HERE THAT THE EXECUTIVE BRANCH HAS NO CONSTITUTIONAL POWER TO MAKE OR WRITE LAWS, THOUGH IT MAY INFLUENCE OR ENGAGE CONGRESS TO DO SO.

EXCEPT BY WIELDING THE VETO POWER, WHICH CONGRESS CAN OVERRIDE, THE EXECUTIVE BRANCH IS OBLIGATED TO WORK WITH WHATEVER LEGISLATORS PASS ALONG. THINK OF IT LIKE THIS: IN A SIMILAR WAY, THE POLICE DO NOT MAKE THE LAWS THEY ENFORCE.

LIKEWISE, CONGRESS HAS NO POWER TO PROSECUTE ITS OWN LAWS, NO MORE THAN A COUNTY SUPERVISOR HAS THE POWER TO TICKET A JAYWALKER OR INVESTIGATE A ROBBERY.

*THE FRAMERS ADDED THIS REQUIREMENT SO THAT WEALTHY EUROPEAN ROYALTY WOULDN'T CROSS THE OCEAN AND USE MONEY AND INFLUENCE TO TAKE POWER AT THE HIGHEST LEVELS. THERE ARE RUMORS THAT THE MEMBERS OF THE CONFEDERATION CONGRESS ITSELF SOUGHT TO BRING PRINCE HENRY OF PRUSSIA TO SERVE AS AMERICA'S "CONSTITUTIONAL MONARCH."

KEEP IN MIND, TO MANY OF THOSE WHO WROTE THE CONSTITUTION, GIVING REGULAR PEOPLE TOO MUCH POWER...

...WOULD MEAN PUTTING THE NEW COUNTRY AT THE MERCY OF "MOB RULE."

...DEMOCRACIES HAVE EVER BEEN SPECTACLES OF TURBULENCE AND CONTENTION...

PLUS, IN THE LATE 18TH CENTURY, TRAVEL WAS ONLY BY HORSE OR BOAT. ALSO, MEN WERE LARGELY JUDGED BY THEIR REPUTATIONS INSIDE A SMALL CIRCLE OF PEERS. A MAJORITY OF THE FRAMERS HELD THAT THE VOTING PUBLIC COULD BE EXPECTED TO SEND LOCAL LEADERS TO THE HOUSE OF REPRESENTATIVES, BUT UNDERSTANDING NATIONAL ISSUES AND ELECTING THE BEST CANDIDATE FOR PRESIDENT WAS AN ENTIRELY DIFFERENT MATTER.

WHAT'S MORE, BOOKS AND LOCAL NEWSPAPERS WERE THE ONLY FORMS OF MEDIA.

WITHOUT MORE MODERN WAYS TO CONVEY PEOPLE AND IDEAS, NATIONAL ELECTIONS WERE ALSO IMPRACTICAL.

EARLY FORMS OF THE INTERNET: 1970S.

FIRST MODERN RAIL TRANSPORT: 1810S.

SAMUEL MORSE'S TELEGRAPH: 1830S.

FIRST TELEPHONE PATENTS: 1870S.

BEGINNING OF RADIO COMMUNICATION: 1890S.

RISE OF COMMERCIAL TELEVISION: 1930S.

O THIS IDEA...

THE POPULATION
HOLE COULDN'T
HOULDN'T ELECT
E PRESIDENT.

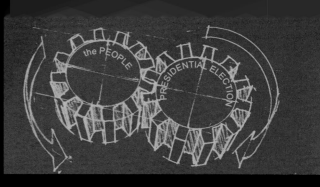

DAY, WHILE
THINK WE
S FOR THE
OFFICE...

OTE
O THEN
IDENT
ARATE
THAT
EKS
DAY.

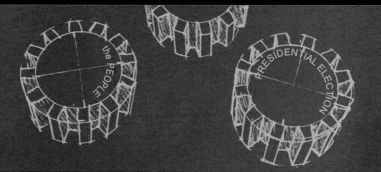

LE"
NLY
OTE.

EARS
BUT
HO
ICAL
S AND
MBIA,
OWN
L

PRESIDENT IS
POPULAR VOTE.

HOW MEMBERS OF THE ELECTORAL COLLEGE ARE
CHOSEN IS UP TO EACH STATE. ORIGINALLY, IN
SOME STATES ELECTORS WERE PICKED BY THE
PEOPLE, IN OTHERS, BY THE STATE LEGISLATURES.
TODAY SERVING AS AN ELECTOR IS AN HONOR
TYPICALLY GIVEN TO ACTIVE AND HIGHLY REGARDED
MEMBERS OF POLITICAL PARTIES.

*ARTICLE II IS CLEAR ON THIS: TO HELP KEEP THINGS FAIR, NO
ONE HOLDING FEDERAL OFFICE OR WORKING FOR THE FEDERAL
GOVERNMENT MAY BE A MEMBER OF THE ELECTORAL COLLEGE

EACH STATE GETS AS MANY ELECTORS AS IT HAS MEMBERS OF CONGRESS. INCLUDING 3 PROVIDED FOR WASHINGTON, D.C., THE TOTAL IS 538.

THE PRESIDENTIAL ELECTION PLAYS OUT STATE BY STATE. IN EACH, THE POLITICAL PARTY THAT WINS HAS ALL THAT STATE'S ELECTORS CAST THEIR BALLOTS FOR PRESIDENT* AND SENDS THEM TO WASHINGTON.

PENNSYLVANIA ELEC. for ROOSEVELT

*EXCEPT, CURRENTLY, FOR MAINE AND NEBRASKA, WHICH HAVE SYSTEMS OF SPLITTING ELECTORAL VOTES. OTHER STATES, TOO, ARE DEBATING DROPPING THEIR WINNER-TAKE-ALL SYSTEMS.

THE ELECTORAL COLLEGE IS STILL WITH US, BUT THERE ARE MAJOR DIFFERENCES BETWEEN THE FIRST PRESIDENTIAL ELECTIONS AND TODAY'S.

IN THE FIRST FOUR ELECTIONS WE ELECTORS COULD VOTE HOWEVER WE WANTED, NEVER MIND THE OPINION OF OUR STATE'S CITIZENS...

...AND WE EACH CAST TWO VOTES, FOR TWO DIFFERENT CANDIDATES. HERE'S ONE FOR ADAMS...

...AND ONE FOR JEFFERSON.

IN THE FINAL TALLY, AS LONG AS ONE CANDIDATE WON A CLEAR MAJORITY, HE WOULD BE PRESIDENT. AND THE RUNNER-UP? VICE PRESIDENT.

AS WE SHALL SEE LATER, THIS ARRANGEMENT DIDN'T LAST.

TODAY'S ELECTORS CAST SINGLE VOTES AND ARE EXPECTED TO RUBBER-STAMP THE WINNER OF THEIR STATE'S CHOICE FOR PRESIDENT AND VICE PRESIDENT.

YET NEITHER THE CONSTITUTION NOR OTHER FEDERAL LAW FORCES ELECTORS TO COMPLY WITH THE MAJORITY PICK.

STILL, THE SO-CALLED *FAITHLESS ELECTORS*—LIKE THE 1972 REPUBLICAN ELECTOR FROM VIRGINIA ROGER LEA MACBRIDE—HAVE NEVER YET CHANGED THE OUTCOME OF AN ELECTION.

AS WITH THE BICAMERAL SYSTEM AND THE THREE-FIFTHS COMPROMISE, ANOTHER REASON FOR THE INVENTION OF THE ELECTORAL COLLEGE WAS TO HELP BALANCE THE POWER OF BIG AND SMALL STATES...

...AND PROSLAVERY AND ANTISLAVERY FACTIONS.

BECAUSE PRESIDENTIAL ELECTIONS ALL COME DOWN TO STATE-BY-STATE ELECTORAL COLLEGE NUMBERS, FOUR TIMES IN OUR HISTORY CANDIDATES HAVE LOST THE PRESIDENCY EVEN AFTER WINNING THE POPULAR VOTE.

ANDREW JACKSON, 1824.

SAMUEL TILDEN, 1876.

GROVER CLEVELAND, 1888.

AL GORE, 2000.

TO WIN THE PRESIDENCY, A CANDIDATE MUST RECEIVE A MAJORITY OF ELECTORAL COLLEGE VOTES—AT LEAST **50% PLUS ONE VOTE.** NOT JUST MORE THAN ANY OTHER CANDIDATE!

WITH ONLY TWO CONTENDERS IN A RACE—SAY, ONE REPUBLICAN VERSUS ONE DEMOCRAT—A CLEAR MAJORITY WILL ALMOST ALWAYS EMERGE.

BUT WHAT IF SEVERAL CANDIDATES ALL MAKE A STRONG SHOWING AND SPLIT THE VOTE SO THAT NO MAJORITY IS POSSIBLE?

DING DING DING

WINNER...!

W-WHA...?

THAT IS EXACTLY WHAT HAPPENED IN THE ELECTION OF 1824.

ANDREW JACKSON, WHO WON THE POPULAR VOTE *AND* RECEIVED THE MOST ELECTORAL COLLEGE VOTES IN THAT CONTEST, LOST IN 1824.

CORRUPT BARGAIN!

AND ARTICLE II OF THE CONSTITUTION DECLARES THAT BY ONE-VOTE-PER-STATE BALLOT, THE HOUSE OF REPRESENTATIVES PICKS THE PRESIDENT, AND THE SENATE THE VICE PRESIDENT.

WINNER OF 1825 HOUSE VOTE FOR PRESIDENT, JOHN QUINCY ADAMS.
WINNER OF 1825 SENATE VOTE FOR VICE PRESIDENT, JOHN C. CALHOUN.

SINCE THERE IS NOTHING TO STOP THIS FROM HAPPENING AGAIN, SOME WOULD CALL THIS A SERIOUS FLAW IN THE SYSTEM.

SHOULD THE PRESIDENT DIE, RESIGN, OR BE REMOVED FROM OFFICE BY CONGRESS, THE VICE PRESIDENT TAKES OVER...

...AND, LIKE ANY OTHER PRESIDENT, TAKES THE OATH OF OFFICE THE FRAMERS COMPOSED.

"I DO SOLEMNLY SWEAR THAT I WILL FAITHFULLY EXECUTE THE OFFICE OF PRESIDENT OF THE UNITED STATES, AND WILL TO THE BEST OF MY ABILITY PRESERVE, PROTECT, AND DEFEND THE CONSTITUTION OF THE UNITED STATES."

WHY IS THIS OATH OF OFFICE SO IMPORTANT? BECAUSE ANYONE WHO TAKES IT PROMISES TO UPHOLD THE CONSTITUTION...EVEN IF HE OR SHE PERSONALLY DOES NOT AGREE WITH EVERY PART OF IT. THE PRESIDENT NEVER HAS THE POWER TO CHANGE OR IGNORE THE CONSTITUTION.

BENJAMIN FRANKLIN ASSERTED THE PRESIDENT SHOULD WORK FOR FREE.

WE DO NOT SOW THE SEEDS OF CONTENTION, FACTION, AND TUMULT, BY MAKING OUR POSTS OF HONOR, PLACES OF PROFIT.

BUT ARTICLE II INSURES THAT THE POSITION IS A PAID ONE. FRANKLIN'S IDEA MAY HAVE BEEN HIGH-MINDED, BUT A PRESIDENTIAL SALARY—CURRENTLY $400,000 PER YEAR (WHICH THE SITTING CONGRESS CANNOT RAISE OR LOWER)—WAS MEANT TO HELP INSURE THAT NOT JUST RICH PEOPLE WOULD SEEK THE OFFICE. THE SALARY, AND A CONSTITUTIONAL ORDER THAT THE PRESIDENT MUST NOT ACCEPT VALUABLE GIFTS FROM THE GOVERN- MENT OR FROM INDIVIDUAL STATES, ALSO HELPS KEEP THE OFFICE IMPARTIAL, FREE FROM FINANACIAL CORRUPTION.

AS WE HAVE SEEN, THE PRESIDENT IS COMMANDER IN CHIEF OF ALL THE ARMED FORCES.

REMEMBER, ARTICLE I GIVES CONGRESS THE POWER TO DECLARE WAR. BUT CONGRESS GOES IN AND OUT OF SESSION. PLUS, ITS ACTIONS COME ONLY AFTER DELIBERATION, COMPROMISE, AND VOTES.

ON THE OTHER HAND, THE EXECUTIVE BRANCH IS ALWAYS ON DUTY. IN EXERCISING CONSTITUTIONAL POWERS, THE PRESIDENT CAN ACT QUICKLY. HIS POWER TO MAKE WAR ASSURES THERE CAN BE A MILITARY RESPONSE TO EMERGENCIES.

YET THE PRESIDENT REMAINS A CIVILIAN.

THIS REFLECTS THE FRAMERS' STAUNCH BELIEF THAT THE COUNTRY MUST NEVER BE RULED BY THE MILITARY.

CONGRESS CONTROLS HOW MUCH MONEY GOES TO THE ARMED FORCES AND THEIR OPERATIONS.

AGAIN, WITH THESE OVERLAPPING *WAR POWERS*, THERE IS ALWAYS THE POTENTIAL TO BRING THESE TWO BRANCHES OF GOVERNMENT INTO A CONFLICT.

EXCEPT IN CASES OF FEDERAL OFFICERS' BEING IMPEACHED, THE PRESIDENT ALSO HAS THE SOLE POWER TO GRANT *REPRIEVES* AND *PARDONS.*

ANYONE WHO HAS BROKEN ANY FEDERAL LAW CAN BE SET FREE SIMPLY AT THE PRESIDENT'S WILL.

SOMEONE CONVICTED ON TYPICAL MURDER CHARGES—STATE LAW—WOULD BE BEYOND THE REACH OF A PRESIDENTIAL PARDON.

RRRRH: RRRRH: K

MANY PRESIDENTIAL PARDONS HAVE BEEN HIGH-PROFILE AND CONTROVERSIAL.

PRESIDENT ANDREW JOHNSON PARDONS CONFEDERATE GENERAL ALBERT PIKE, ACCUSED OF TREASON, IN 1865.

RICHARD NIXON PARDONS THE UNION ORGANIZER JIMMY HOFFA, CONVICTED OF ATTEMPTED BRIBERY, IN 1971.

SUCCESSOR GERALD FORD PARDONS RESIGNED PRESIDENT RICHARD NIXON FOR THE WATERGATE SCANDAL, IN 1974.

GEORGE H. W. BUSH PARDONS HIS SECRETARY OF DEFENSE, CASPAR WEINBERGER, FOR LYING TO INVESTIGATORS ABOUT THE *IRAN-CONTRA SCANDAL,* IN 1992.

BILL CLINTON PARDONS THE BILLIONAIRE BUSINESSMAN MARC RICH FOR TAX EVASION AND ILLEGAL OIL TRADING WITH IRAN, IN 2001.

AS THE CHIEF EXECUTIVE, THE PRESIDENT IS THE FACE THE UNITED STATES SHOWS TO THE REST OF THE WORLD.

ACCORDINGLY, THE PRESIDENT HAS THE POWER TO MAKE *TREATIES,* AGREEMENTS WITH OTHER COUNTRIES...

...BUT BEFORE THEY CAN BECOME LAW, THE SENATE MUST APPROVE, OR *RATIFY,* THEM BY A 2/3 MAJORITY.*

*ANOTHER EXAMPLE OF CHECKS AND BALANCES.

AUTHORIZED BY A TREATY RATIFIED BY THE SENATE IN 1821, THE UNITED STATES BOUGHT FLORIDA—AND THE GULF COASTS OF ALABAMA AND MISSISSIPPI—FROM SPAIN.

FLORIDA TERRITORY

THE CONSTITUTION GIVES THE PRESIDENT THE AUTHORITY TO APPOINT...

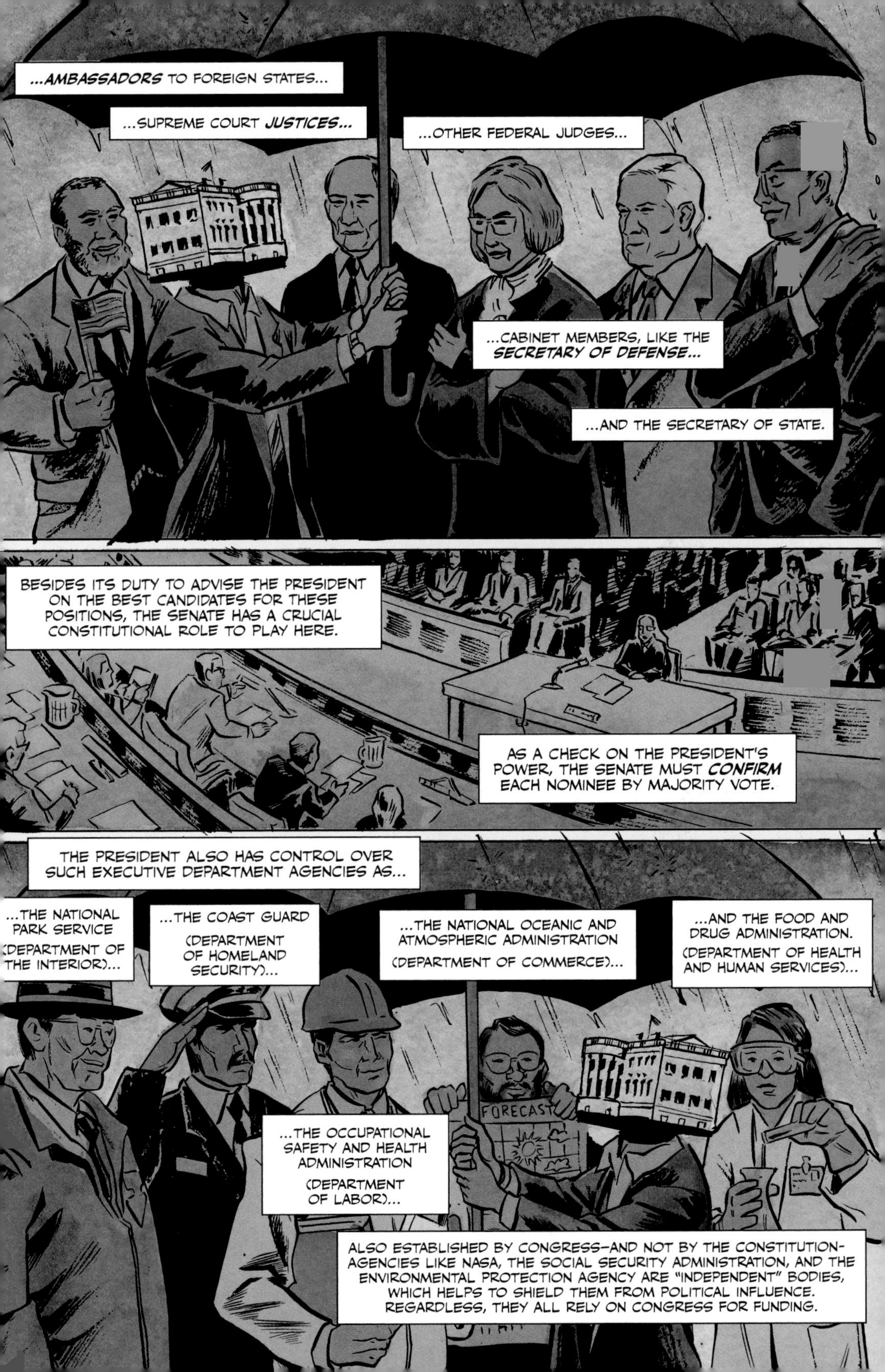

...AMBASSADORS TO FOREIGN STATES...
...SUPREME COURT JUSTICES...
...OTHER FEDERAL JUDGES...
...CABINET MEMBERS, LIKE THE SECRETARY OF DEFENSE...
...AND THE SECRETARY OF STATE.
BESIDES ITS DUTY TO ADVISE THE PRESIDENT ON THE BEST CANDIDATES FOR THESE POSITIONS, THE SENATE HAS A CRUCIAL CONSTITUTIONAL ROLE TO PLAY HERE.
AS A CHECK ON THE PRESIDENT'S POWER, THE SENATE MUST CONFIRM EACH NOMINEE BY MAJORITY VOTE.
THE PRESIDENT ALSO HAS CONTROL OVER SUCH EXECUTIVE DEPARTMENT AGENCIES AS...
...THE NATIONAL PARK SERVICE (DEPARTMENT OF THE INTERIOR)...
...THE COAST GUARD (DEPARTMENT OF HOMELAND SECURITY)...
...THE NATIONAL OCEANIC AND ATMOSPHERIC ADMINISTRATION (DEPARTMENT OF COMMERCE)...
...AND THE FOOD AND DRUG ADMINISTRATION. (DEPARTMENT OF HEALTH AND HUMAN SERVICES)...
FORECAST
...THE OCCUPATIONAL SAFETY AND HEALTH ADMINISTRATION (DEPARTMENT OF LABOR)...
ALSO ESTABLISHED BY CONGRESS—AND NOT BY THE CONSTITUTION—AGENCIES LIKE NASA, THE SOCIAL SECURITY ADMINISTRATION, AND THE ENVIRONMENTAL PROTECTION AGENCY ARE "INDEPENDENT" BODIES, WHICH HELPS TO SHIELD THEM FROM POLITICAL INFLUENCE. REGARDLESS, THEY ALL RELY ON CONGRESS FOR FUNDING.

ARTICLE II REQUIRES THE PRESIDENT TO DELIVER **STATE OF THE UNION** REPORTS TO CONGRESS, TO EXPRESS PLANS FOR THE COUNTRY'S FUTURE.

MODERN CUSTOM IS TO DO THIS IN PERSON ANNUALLY.

THE COUNTRY, I AM THANKFUL TO SAY, IS AT PEACE WITH ALL THE WORLD, AND MANY HAPPY MANIFESTATIONS MULTIPLY ABOUT US OF A GROWING CORDIALITY AND SENSE OF COMMUNITY OF INTEREST AMONG THE NATIONS, FORESHADOWING AN AGE OF SETTLED PEACE AND GOOD WILL.

PRESIDENT WOODROW WILSON (1913–1921).

AS ANOTHER FORM OF CHECKS AND BALANCES, THE PRESIDENT HAS THE POWER TO CALL **SPECIAL SESSIONS** OF CONGRESS, COMPELLING IT TO MEET AND TAKE ACTION IN RESPONSE TO EMERGENCIES.

HE MAY ALSO SEND CONGRESS HOME IF ITS TWO CHAMBERS CANNOT AGREE ON A DATE TO ADJOURN.

Article III.

ARTICLE III OF THE CONSTITUTION ESTABLISHES THE POWERS AND RESPONSIBILITIES OF THE THIRD BRANCH OF GOVERNMENT...

...THE *JUDICIARY*.

IT IS NOT JUST THE *SUPREME COURT OF THE UNITED STATES* THAT MAKES UP THE JUDICIAL BRANCH. ARTICLE III MAY SPECIFICALLY ESTABLISH THE SUPREME COURT, BUT IT ALSO EMPOWERS CONGRESS TO FORM OUR ENTIRE SYSTEM OF LOWER, OR *INFERIOR*, FEDERAL COURTS.

THESE COURTS DECIDE ALL MATTERS OF FEDERAL LAW, *CIVIL* AND *CRIMINAL*. ALL CASES THAT ARISE FROM THE CONSTITUTION, AND FROM ACTIONS TAKEN BY ALL THREE BRANCHES OF GOVERNMENT, ARE HEARD HERE...

...WITH THE SUPREME COURT HAVING THE FINAL SAY.

THE DUTY OF THE JUDICIAL BRANCH IS TO APPLY AND INTERPRET THE LAW, TO DEFINE THE LAW'S TRUE MEANING...

...AND, ULTIMATELY, TO INSURE THAT JUSTICE IS DONE.

CITIZENS PLAY AN ABSOLUTELY ESSENTIAL, DIRECT ROLE IN THIS BRANCH OF GOVERNMENT...

...BY SERVING ON *JURIES*.

SPELLED OUT MORE CLEARLY IN THE *BILL OF RIGHTS*, ARTICLE III ENSURES THAT "WE, THE PEOPLE" HAVE AN IMPORTANT CHECK AND BALANCE AGAINST GOVERNMENT OFFICERS—JUDGES—BY STATING THAT ALL CRIMES SHALL BE TRIED BY JURY. ONLY IN IMPEACHMENT CASES DO CITIZENS NOT HAVE THIS RIGHT. THAT'S WHY JURY SERVICE IS AS IMPERATIVE AS VOTING.

TODAY, JUST AS BEFORE THE CONSTITUTION CAME INTO EFFECT, EVERY STATE HAS ITS OWN LAWS AND ITS OWN COURT SYSTEM.

BY FAR MOST LEGAL CASES PLAY OUT IN STATE COURTS.

THE DISORDERLY TIMES OF THE ARTICLES OF CONFEDERATION MADE IT CLEAR TO THE FRAMERS THAT A PACK OF SEPARATE BUT EQUAL STATE COURTS COULD RESULT ONLY IN ANARCHY.

ALEXANDER HAMILTON SAID THAT TOGETHER THEY WOULD BE LIKE A *HYDRA,* A MYTHOLOGICAL MONSTER WITH MANY HEADS.

THERE NEEDED TO BE A HIGHER AUTHORITY— A REFEREE—OVER ALL OF THEM...

...AND SO THE NATIONAL JUDICIARY BRANCH WAS BORN.

ALTHOUGH THE SUPREME COURT STARTED OUT WITH SIX PEOPLE, TODAY IT HAS GROWN TO NINE, ONE *CHIEF JUSTICE* AND EIGHT *ASSOCIATE JUSTICES.*

APPOINTED BY THE PRESIDENT AND CONFIRMED BY THE SENATE, FEDERAL JUDGES SERVE "DURING GOOD BEHAVIOR" UNTIL THEY RESIGN, DIE, OR ARE IMPEACHED AND REMOVED FROM OFFICE.

FOR THE SUPREME COURT OF THE UNITED STATES, CONGRESS HAS THE POWER TO SET THE NUMBER OF JUSTICES AS IT SEES FIT.

SINCE 1869, THAT TOTAL HAS BEEN FIXED AT NINE.

CRIMINAL CASES THAT ARE MATTERS OF FEDERAL LAW AND ARE THEREFORE TRIED IN ARTICLE III COURTS INCLUDE...

...DRUG SMUGGLING...

...BANK ROBBERY...

...COUNTERFEITING...

...CRIMES COMMITTED AT SEA.

NOTE THAT EVEN MANY SERIOUS CRIMES, LIKE MURDER, RAPE, AND BURGLARY (UNLESS WITH CLEAR CONNECTIONS TO THE FEDERAL GOVERNMENT), ARE MATTERS FOR STATE, NOT FEDERAL, COURT.

EXAMPLES OF CIVIL CASES TRIED IN FEDERAL COURT ARE...

...COPYRIGHT AND PATENT INFRINGEMENT...

OLLIE'S BBQ

...CIVIL RIGHTS CASES...

...BANKRUPTCY.

IT IS IN THE FEDERAL COURT SYSTEM THAT ONE STATE CAN SUE ANOTHER, WHERE CITIZENS OF DIFFERENT STATES GO TO SETTLE DISPUTES*...

*IF THE DOLLAR AMOUNT IN CONTENTION EXCEEDS $75,000—AS IS OFTEN THE CASE WHEN INDIVIDUALS SUE CORPORATIONS IN *PRODUCT LIABILITY* CASES.

SUMMONS

...AND WHERE FEDERAL OFFICEHOLDERS, FOREIGN GOVERNMENTS, AND THEIR AGENTS...

...AND EVEN THE UNITED STATES ITSELF CAN BE SUED.

WHEN THE VERY LAWS AND ACTS OF CONGRESS OR THE STATES ARE TO BE CHALLENGED...

...AND WITH THIS BILL I, AS GOVERNOR, HAVE JUST SIGNED... ...MY CONSTITUENTS WILL NOW USE THESE BADGER BUCKS INSTEAD OF U.S. DOLLARS!

...THAT, TOO, IS THE DOMAIN OF THE FEDERAL COURTS.

CRACK
CRACK

NOT SO FAST, WISCONSIN!

UNDER ARTICLE I, SECTION 8, CLAUSE 5 OF THE CONSTITUTION, ONLY THE U.S. CONGRESS HAS THE POWER TO COIN MONEY!

THE JUDICIARY BRANCH—AND, ULTIMATELY, THE SUPREME COURT—HAVE AN EXTRAORDINARY POWER... THE POWER TO DECIDE IF A LAW OR AN ACT OF GOVERNMENT CONFLICTS WITH THE CONSTITUTION ITSELF AND TO STRIKE IT DOWN IF IT DOES.

THIS IS CALLED JUDICIAL REVIEW, AND IT CAN OVERRIDE THE WILL OF A CITIZEN, A STATE GOVERNMENT, CONGRESS, THE PRESIDENT, EVEN A MAJORITY OF THE PEOPLE. JUDICIAL REVIEW, OR THE LICENSE TO INTERPRET THE CONSTITUTION, IS PROBABLY THE BEST-KNOWN GRANT OF POWER BY THE PEOPLE TO THE JUDICIAL BRANCH.

BUT...IT IS IMPORTANT TO REALIZE THAT THIS POWER IS NOT EXPRESSLY WRITTEN INTO THE CONSTITUTION.

IT IS INSTEAD THE LEGACY OF TWO HISTORICAL CONFLICTS...

...A DRAMATIC PRESIDENTIAL ELECTION...

...AND A SUPREME COURT CASE.

PRIOR TO THE ELECTION OF 1800, BITTERLY OPPOSED POLITICAL PARTIES HAD FORMED AND WERE CLASHING OVER WHAT DIRECTION THE COUNTRY'S FUTURE SHOULD TAKE.

DEMOCRATIC REPUBLICAN PARTY

FEDERALIST PARTY

BECAUSE OF AN ELECTORAL TIE, CONGRESS HAD TO CHOOSE THE PRESIDENT AND VICE PRESIDENT.

BUT ONE THING WAS CLEAR: THE SITTING PRESIDENT, JOHN ADAMS, AND HIS PARTY, THE *FEDERALISTS*, WERE THROWN OUT.

ON THE LAST NIGHT OF HIS PRESIDENCY ADAMS TOOK ONE LAST SHOT AT KEEPING HIS PARTY'S IDEAS ALIVE.

MR. PRESIDENT! HURRY! IT'S NEARLY MIDNIGHT!

WHILE HE STILL HAD THE POWER, HE WANTED TO APPOINT AS MANY JUDGES LOYAL TO THE FEDERALIST PARTY AS HE COULD.

SIGNED DOCUMENTS CALLED *COMMISSIONS* HAD TO BE DELIVERED TO MAKE THESE APPOINTMENTS OFFICIAL.

ONE MAN EAGERLY EXPECTING ONE OF THESE COMMISSIONS WAS *WILLIAM MARBURY*.

BUT SOMEHOW, MARBURY'S COMMISSION NEVER WENT OUT THAT NIGHT.

THOMAS JEFFERSON WAS THE NEW PRESIDENT. HE MADE JAMES MADISON HIS SECRETARY OF STATE...

AND BECAUSE FEDERALISTS LIKE MARBURY WERE THE POLITICAL ENEMIES OF THE NEW MEN IN CHARGE...

WHERE IS THAT BLOODY COMMISSION?

...MADISON DECIDED NOT TO DELIVER IT AT ALL...

...AND MARBURY SUED TO TRY TO FORCE HIM TO GIVE IT UP.

DO YOU HEAR ME, MADISON? I'M TAKING THIS TO THE SUPREME COURT!

EARLIER AN ACT OF CONGRESS HAD GIVEN THE SUPREME COURT THE POWER TO TAKE IMMEDIATELY CERTAIN CASES, OF THOSE WANTING A WAY TO LEGALLY FORCE GOVERNMENT OFFICIALS TO DO THEIR JOBS.

HMM...

Original Jurisdiction Writs of Mandamus

JOHN MARSHALL WAS THE CHIEF JUSTICE OF THE UNITED STATES AT THE TIME...

AND EVEN THOUGH IT WAS DECIDED THAT MARBURY DID HAVE A RIGHT TO HIS COMMISSION...

If courts are to regard the Constitution, and the Constitution is superior to any ordinary act of legislature, the Constituti... and not such ordinary act, must gover... ...case to which they both apply.

...MARSHALL ASSERTED THAT THE SUPREME COURT DID NOT HAVE THE AUTHORITY TO GRANT IT TO HIM. WHY? BECAUSE THE CONSTITUTION DOESN'T SAY THAT THE JUDICIAL BRANCH CAN DO THAT.

EXCEPT IN RARE INSTANCES,* THE SUPREME COURT IS AN *APPELLATE COURT.* ONE CANNOT TAKE A CASE STRAIGHT TO IT.

SORRY, I CANNOT ACCEPT.

*LIKE A STATE SUING ANOTHER STATE OR CASES INVOLVING "AMBASSADORS, OTHER PUBLIC MINISTERS, AND CONSULS."

SO IN GIVING UP ONE POWER, THE JUDICIARY TOOK ANOTHER FOR ITS OWN.

THE CONSTITUTION ITSELF IS A HIGHER AUTHORITY THAN CONGRESS...

...OR ANY LOWER GOVERNMENT.

JUDICIAL REVIEW IS ANOTHER INSTANCE OF CHECKS AND BALANCES IN OUR GOVERNMENT.

BECAUSE OF THIS, IMPORTANT, OR *LANDMARK*, SUPREME COURT CASES HAVE SHAPED HOW WE UNDERSTAND AND IMPLEMENT OUR LAWS AND GOVERNMENT.

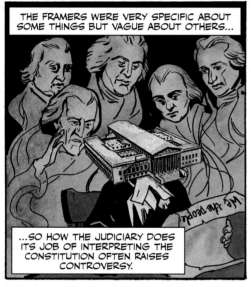

THE FRAMERS WERE VERY SPECIFIC ABOUT SOME THINGS BUT VAGUE ABOUT OTHERS...

...SO HOW THE JUDICIARY DOES ITS JOB OF INTERPRETING THE CONSTITUTION OFTEN RAISES CONTROVERSY.

THERE MAY BE MANY GRAY AREAS.

"BUT JUSTICES CANNOT SIT AROUND, RULING ON THE CONSTITUTIONALITY OF IMAGINARY LEGAL PROBLEMS."

OH. SHOOT.

THE SUPREME COURT CAN HEAR ONLY CASES FROM ENTITIES GENUINELY ABLE TO PROVE A GOVERNMENT ACTION HAS HARMED THEM.

SOME ARGUE THAT THE CONSTITUTION IS A LIVING DOCUMENT, AND THAT HOW WE LOOK AT IT SHOULD DEPEND ON HOW WE LIVE TODAY.

OPPOSING THIS VIEW, ORIGINALISTS ASSERT THAT ALL THAT MATTERS IS WHAT THE FRAMERS, IN 1787, INTENDED THE CONSTITUTION TO MEAN.

THE FRAMERS CONSIDERED ONLY ONE CRIME SO HEINOUS THAT IT HAD TO BE MENTIONED EXPLICITLY IN THE CONSTITUTION.

TREASON

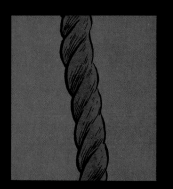

TREASON IS THE CRIME OF TAKING UP ARMS AGAINST THE UNITED STATES AND/OR PROVIDING "AID AND COMFORT" TO ITS ENEMIES DURING A TIME OF DECLARED WAR...

SERIOUS CRIMES LIKE *ESPIONAGE* AND *SABOTAGE* ARE NOT NECESSARILY *TREASON*.

...AND NO ONE SHALL BE CONVICTED OF TREASON WITHOUT CONFESSING TO THE CRIME OR WITHOUT THE TESTIMONY OF TWO WITNESSES.

BACK IN BRITAIN, TREASON CHARGES COULD GIVE THE KING THE RIGHT TO TAKE ALL OF THE TRAITOR'S PROPERTY, EVEN FROM HIS INNOCENT FAMILY MEMBERS. OFTEN "TRAITORS" WERE SIMPLY PEOPLE WHO CRITICIZED THE GOVERNMENT. A MAN COULD EVEN BE EXECUTED AS A TRAITOR FOR KILLING ONE OF THE KING'S STAGS!

THE FRAMERS WOULD HAVE NONE OF THIS IN THE UNITED STATES. THAT IS WHY WHAT TREASON, AND WHAT ITS PUNISHMENT MAY NOT INCLUDE, ARE SO CAREFULLY DEFINED IN THE CONSTITUTION.

THE UNITED STATES HAS NEVER EXECUTED A TRAITOR.

ARTICLE IV OF THE CONSTITUTION COVERS RELATIONS AMONG THE STATES...

LET ME TAKE YOU UNDER MY WING ON THIS.

...AND BETWEEN THE STATES AND THE NATIONAL GOVERNMENT.

REMEMBER, *FEDERALISM*—THAT STATES HAVE SOME POWERS, AND THE NATIONAL GOVERNMENT OTHERS—IS A CORNERSTONE OF OUR REPUBLIC.

THE FULL FAITH AND CREDIT CLAUSE GUARANTEES THAT CONTRACTS AND LAWS MADE IN ONE STATE ARE VALID IN EVERY OTHER STATE.

MARRIAGES AND ADOPTIONS ARE TWO EXAMPLES.

BUT ONE STATE CANNOT ENFORCE THE CRIMINAL LAWS OF ANOTHER STATE.

CITIZENS HAVE THE RIGHT TO PASS FREELY FROM STATE TO STATE...

THE ARTICLES OF CONFEDERATION ACTUALLY BLOCKED "VAGABONDS" AND "PAUPERS" FROM THIS FREEDOM. THE CONSTITUTION, BY CONTRAST, NEVER DISCRIMINATES BETWEEN RICH AND POOR.

...AND MUST BE AFFORDED ALL THE *"PRIVILEGES AND IMMUNITIES"* STATES RECOGNIZE FOR THEIR OWN PEOPLE.

ALASKA STATE PARK

ALASKANS ONLY!

BUT STATES MAY DISCRIMINATE, FOR EXAMPLE, WHEN IT COMES TO VOTING RIGHTS, PRACTICING LAW OR MEDICINE, OR QUALIFYING FOR REDUCED TUITION AT STATE COLLEGES AND UNIVERSITIES.

FUGITIVES FROM JUSTICE, THOSE CHARGED WITH CRIMES WHO FLEE ACROSS STATE LINES...

1ST BANK

...DON'T GET OFF EASILY IN THE CONSTITUTION.

ARTICLE IV SECTION 2, CLAUSE 2

MISSISSIPPI

ARKANSAS

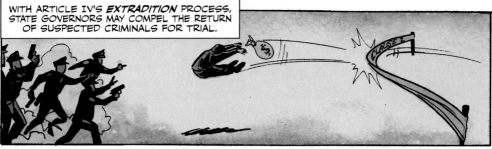

WITH ARTICLE IV'S *EXTRADITION* PROCESS, STATE GOVERNORS MAY COMPEL THE RETURN OF SUSPECTED CRIMINALS FOR TRIAL.

CLAUSE 2

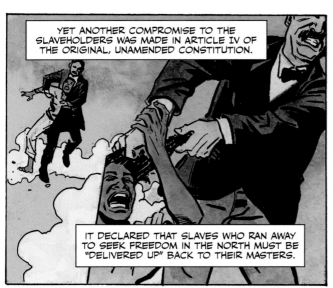

YET ANOTHER COMPROMISE TO THE SLAVEHOLDERS WAS MADE IN ARTICLE IV OF THE ORIGINAL, UNAMENDED CONSTITUTION.

IT DECLARED THAT SLAVES WHO RAN AWAY TO SEEK FREEDOM IN THE NORTH MUST BE "DELIVERED UP" BACK TO THEIR MASTERS.

THIS LAW SPARKED OUTRAGE AMONG ABOLITIONISTS LIKE *WILLIAM LLOYD GARRISON.*

SO PERISH ALL COMPROMISES WITH TYRANNY!

IN 1865 THE THIRTEENTH AMENDMENT MADE THIS PROVISION *NULL AND VOID.*

ARTICLE IV ALSO COVERS HOW CONGRESS (AND ONLY CONGRESS) MAY ADMIT NEW STATES TO THE UNION.

NO NEW STATES MAY FORM IN WHOLE OR IN PART FROM EXISTING STATES WITHOUT THE APPROVAL OF CONGRESS AND THE STATE LEGISLATURES.

SEVERAL STATES HAVE BEEN CREATED THIS WAY: VERMONT, KENTUCKY, TENNESSEE, MAINE, AND WEST VIRGINIA.

NOT ALL OF THE LANDS UNDER THE U.S. FLAG ARE STATES. RIGHT NOW THERE ARE MORE THAN A DOZEN *INSULAR AREAS* OR *TERRITORIES.*

CONGRESS MAKES ALL LAWS FOR THESE PROPERTIES...

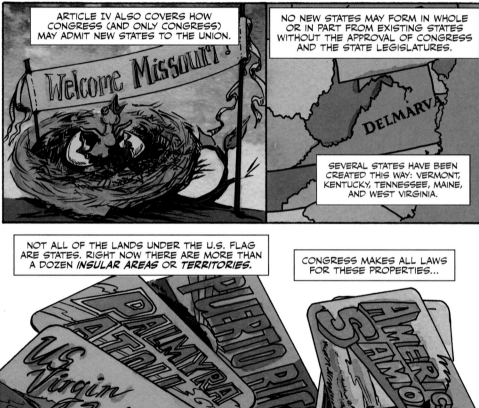

THE PHILIPPINES WAS ONCE A U.S. TERRITORY TOO.

...AS WELL AS FOR CERTAIN AREAS CONTROLLED BY THE U.S. GOVERNMENT WITHIN STATES' BORDERS.

IN THESE PLACES IT MAY CARRY OUT POLICIES WHETHER THE STATES' PEOPLE AGREE WITH THEM...

THIS IS FEDERAL LAND, AND THE WILD FREE-ROAMING HORSES AND BURROS ACT PROTECTS THESE ANIMALS.

Wild Horses

ANIMAL RIGHTS!

...OR NOT.

BUT THIS IS *OUR* STATE! WE DON'T WANT THAT *RADIOACTIVE* WASTE BURIED HERE!

SORRY...

...THIS IS OUR JURISDICTION.

NEVA TEST

ARTICLE IV BINDS THE FEDERAL GOVERNMENT TO PROTECT EACH STATE FROM INVASION AND DOMESTIC UPRISINGS.

WAR OF 1812.

IT ALSO EMPOWERS THE PRESIDENT TO SEND U.S. MARSHALS, THE MILITARY, OR "FEDERALIZED" NATIONAL GUARD TROOPS INTO A STATE TO ENFORCE FEDERAL LAW.

THE CONSTITUTION PROCLAIMS THAT EACH STATE SHALL HAVE "A REPUBLICAN FORM OF GOVERNMENT." BASICALLY, THIS *GUARANTEE CLAUSE* MEANS THAT NO STATE CAN BECOME A MONARCHY OR A DICTATORSHIP, OR ADOPT SOME OTHER FORM OF GOVERNMENT THAT WOULD NOT ALLOW ITS PEOPLE TO VOTE.

I CROWN THEE...

...KING OF NEW HAMPSHIRE.

THE STATE? I *AM* THE STATE!

ARTICLE V OUTLINES HOW THE CONSTITUTION CAN BE *AMENDED*, OR CHANGED.

Are you sure you want to delete the Articles of Confederation?

YES NO

REMEMBER, WHEN THE FRAMERS FIRST WROTE THE CONSTITUTION, THEY WERE TAKING ANOTHER WHOLE GOVERNMENT AND BODY OF LAWS, ONE ONLY SIX YEARS OLD, AND COMPLETELY GETTING RID OF IT.

THEY WERE WISE ENOUGH TO REALIZE THAT THE PEOPLE OF THE NATION MIGHT NEED TO CHANGE OR ADD TO THEIR WORK IN THE FUTURE.

BUT IF AMENDING THE CONSTITUTION WAS TOO EASY...

STEP RIGHT UP! YOU WANT AMENDMENTS? WE GOT AMENDMENTS GALORE!

EASY FINANCING! EASY TERMS!

SIR? HOW ABOUT YOU? YOU LOOK LIKE YOU COULD USE AN AMENDMENT TODAY!

...THEN ALL THE STRUGGLE THAT WENT INTO WRITING IT COULD BE FOR NOTHING.

SO CHANGING THE CONSTITUTION...

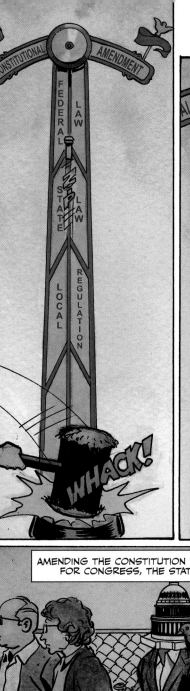

...HAD TO BE MADE HARDER THAN WRITING ANY OTHER KIND OF LAW.

ACTUALLY, PEOPLE HAVE TRIED AND FAILED TO AMEND THE CONSTITUTION OVER 10,000 TIMES.

AMENDING THE CONSTITUTION IS A PROCESS EXCLUSIVELY FOR CONGRESS, THE STATES, AND THE PEOPLE...

...AND NOT THE PRESIDENT OR THE JUDICIAL BRANCH.

NEITHER HAS ANY EXPLICIT POWER TO CHANGE, ADD, OR SUBTRACT SO MUCH AS A SINGLE WORD OF THE DOCUMENT.

IDEAS OR *PROPOSALS* FOR AMENDMENTS MAY BE MADE BY 2/3 OF BOTH HOUSES OF CONGRESS.

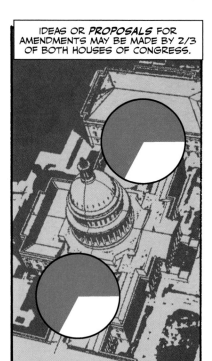

LIKE THE SAME *SUPERMAJORITY* OF LEGISLATORS NEEDED TO OVERRIDE A PRESIDENTIAL VETO.

PHONE

BUT IF 2/3 OF THE STATE GOVERNMENTS AGREE TO AMEND THE CONSTITUTION, THEY CAN BYPASS CONGRESS AND CALL FOR SPECIAL CONVENTIONS TO PROPOSE ONE.*

*SO FAR THIS PROCESS HAS NEVER SUCCESSFULLY BEEN CARRIED OUT.

??? °°

IN EITHER CASE, ARTICLE V SPELLS OUT TWO WAYS AMENDMENTS CAN BE RATIFIED.

NUMBER ONE, BY BEING SENT TO ALL FIFTY STATE LEGISLATURES...

...AND RECEIVING A YES VOTE FROM 3/4 OF THEM.

CONSTITUTIONAL AMENDMENT

NUMBER TWO, BY CALLING SPECIAL CONVENTIONS OF THE PEOPLE IN ALL THE STATES TO VOTE THE AMENDMENT UP OR DOWN.

HERE'S ONE FOR YOU, MA'AM. AND YOU, SIR. AND YOU. AND YOU.

AGAIN, IT WOULD TAKE 3/4 OF THE STATES TO APPROVE.

EITHER WAY, IT WOULD TAKE JUST 13 STATES TO BLOCK ANY AMENDMENT FROM BEING RATIFIED.

TO PRESERVE THE GREAT COMPROMISE, NO AMENDMENT CAN FORCE A STATE TO GIVE UP ITS EQUAL REPRESENTATION IN THE SENATE.

SINCE CONGRESS OR STATE LEGISLATURES ARE SPECIFICALLY INVOLVED IN THE PROCESS, ARTICLE V SPELLS OUT ONLY INDIRECT WAYS FOR "WE, THE PEOPLE" TO AMEND THE CONSTITUTION. BUT THINK ABOUT THIS: THE PREAMBLE AND THE DECLARATION OF INDEPENDENCE BOTH UPHOLD THE RIGHT OF THE PEOPLE TO ESTABLISH, OR ABOLISH, GOVERNMENT. DOES IT FOLLOW THAT ARTICLE V IS JUST ONE OFFICIAL MODE OF AMENDING THE CONSTITUTION?

THE FRAMERS ALSO ADDED A PROMISE THAT NO AMENDMENTS ON THE INSTITUTION OF SLAVERY COULD BE MADE UNTIL, AT THE EARLIEST, 1808.

Article VI.

WITH ARTICLE VI, THE FRAMERS ASSUMED ALL DEBTS THE STATES HAD INCURRED DURING THE REVOLUTIONARY WAR AND UNDER THE ARTICLES OF CONFEDERATION.

IT ALSO DECREES THE CONSTITUTION TO BE "THE SUPREME LAW OF THE LAND."

WITH THIS *SUPREMACY CLAUSE*, IF A STATE OR LOCAL LAW CONFLICTS WITH THE CONSTITUTION, IT IS OVERPOWERED...

...OR, IN OTHER WORDS, *TRUMPED.*

ARTICLE VI HAS ALL WHO HOLD PUBLIC OFFICE, AT EVERY LEVEL IN THE UNITED STATES, SWEAR TO UPHOLD THE CONSTITUTION AHEAD OF ANY OTHER AUTHORITY.

...AGAIN, EVEN IF THEY DISAGREE WITH PARTS OF IT.

AND BECAUSE BLOODY CLASHES BETWEEN RIVAL RELIGIONS HAVE PLAGUED HUMANKIND FOR CENTURIES...

...THE CONSTITUTION MANDATES THAT THERE WILL BE NO "RELIGIOUS TEST" TO HOLD ANY FEDERAL OFFICE.

DAVID LEVY YULEE, FIRST JEW ELECTED TO SENATE, 1845.

JOHN F. KENNEDY, JR., FIRST CATHOLIC ELECTED TO PRESIDENCY, 1960.

KEITH ELLISON, FIRST MUSLIM ELECTED TO CONGRESS, 2006.

MAZZIE HIRONO AND HANK JOHNSON, FIRST BUDDHISTS ELECTED TO CONGRESS, 2006.

REED SMOOT, FIRST MORMON ELECTED TO SENATE, 1902.

LOUIS BRANDEIS, FIRST JEW APPOINTED TO SUPREME COURT OF THE UNITED STATES, 1916.

THE FRAMERS MAY HAVE THOUGHT THEY WERE IMPLYING THIS...

...BUT THE CONSTITUTION MAKES NO EXPRESS REQUIREMENT AS TO RACE OR SEX TO HOLD PUBLIC OFFICE.

CHARLES CURTIS, FIRST NATIVE AMERICAN ELECTED TO SENATE, 1907.

HIRAM REVELS, FIRST AFRICAN-AMERICAN ELECTED TO SENATE, 1870.

JOSEPH HAYNE RAINEY, FIRST AFRICAN-AMERICAN ELECTED TO THE HOUSE, 1870.

OCTAVIO LARRAZOLO, FIRST HISPANIC ELECTED TO SENATE, 1928.

HATTIE OPHELIA WYATT CARAWAY, FIRST WOMAN ELECTED TO SENATE, 1932.

Article. VII.

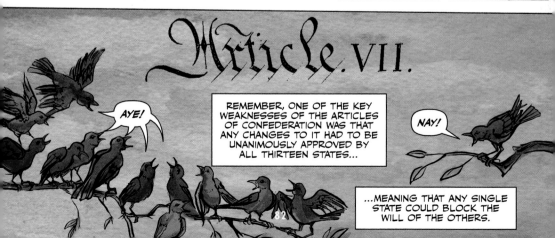

AYE!

REMEMBER, ONE OF THE KEY WEAKNESSES OF THE ARTICLES OF CONFEDERATION WAS THAT ANY CHANGES TO IT HAD TO BE UNANIMOUSLY APPROVED BY ALL THIRTEEN STATES...

NAY!

...MEANING THAT ANY SINGLE STATE COULD BLOCK THE WILL OF THE OTHERS.

SO ARTICLE VII MADE THE ACCEPTANCE OF NINE OF THE ORIGINAL THIRTEEN STATES NECESSARY FOR THE CONSTITUTION TO BECOME LAW.

AND BECAUSE THE CONFEDERATION CONGRESS WOULD HAVE BEEN SIGNING ITSELF OUT OF EXISTENCE...

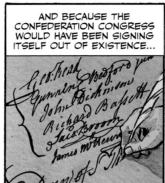

...AND STATE LEGISLATURES GIVING UP MUCH OF THEIR POWER...

...THE CONSTITUTION WAS DESIGNED TO BE EITHER EMBRACED OR REJECTED NOT, ULTIMATELY, BY THOSE AUTHORITIES...

...BUT BY THE PEOPLE.

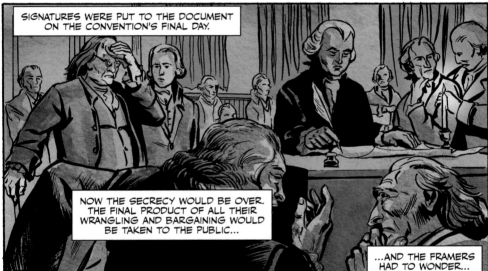

SIGNATURES WERE PUT TO THE DOCUMENT ON THE CONVENTION'S FINAL DAY.

NOW THE SECRECY WOULD BE OVER. THE FINAL PRODUCT OF ALL THEIR WRANGLING AND BARGAINING WOULD BE TAKEN TO THE PUBLIC...

...AND THE FRAMERS HAD TO WONDER...

...WHAT WOULD THE PEOPLE DO WITH IT?

CLINK

THE CONVENTION DELEGATES WHO SIGNED THE CONSTITUTION READIED FOR THEIR NEXT STEP...

COME, COME, BROTHER JAMES! MUST WE GROVEL BEFORE YOU TOAST WITH US?

AH...ALL THE ACRIMONY HAS SOURED MY STOMACH.

ALEXANDER, BOTH YOUR NEW YORK COLLEAGUES QUIT IN PROTEST. THEN WE HAVE RANDOLPH'S EXIT. MASON'S EXIT...

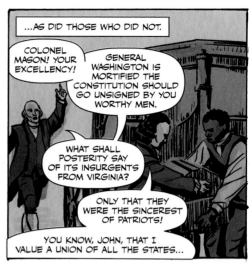

...AS DID THOSE WHO DID NOT.

COLONEL MASON! YOUR EXCELLENCY!

GENERAL WASHINGTON IS MORTIFIED THE CONSTITUTION SHOULD GO UNSIGNED BY YOU WORTHY MEN.

WHAT SHALL POSTERITY SAY OF ITS INSURGENTS FROM VIRGINIA?

ONLY THAT THEY WERE THE SINCEREST OF PATRIOTS!

YOU KNOW, JOHN, THAT I VALUE A UNION OF ALL THE STATES...

MASON? GOOD RIDDANCE. IF ONLY HE'D HAD LESS LUCK WITH HIS CARRIAGE WRECK THAN I WITH MINE!

AMERICA IS TO BE A GREAT EMPIRE. OF MANUFACTURING AND COMMERCE! I DID NOT LEAD MY CHARGE AT YORKTOWN TO KEEP THESE PRECIOUS STATES AND PETTY FARMERS INVIOLABLE!

...

ER, INDEED. BUT THE POPULARITY OF OUR PLAN IS NOT FULLY KNOWN. HOW BEST MAY WE APPEAL TO THE PEOPLE TO RATIFY?

...BUT THE INDECENT MANNER IN WHICH BUSINESS WAS CONDUCTED THESE LAST WEEKS! YOU, SIR, READ MY OBJECTIONS...

...THE ABOMINATION OF SLAVERY RETAINED! A TYRANT PRESIDENT! AN ARISTOCRATIC SENATE! WITH A STANDING ARMY TO FEND FOR THEM!

FOR THAT, MY FRIEND, OUR PENS SHALL BE OUR SWORDS. WE SHALL CALL OURSELVES PUBLIUS.

HMM?

MYSELF, YOU, AND MR. MORRIS HERE. WE SHALL MAKE OUR CASE WITH OUR INTELLECT AND POWERS OF PERSUASION, IN THE GUISE OF A SINGLE PERSONA.

NOT I, GENTLEMEN. THE WINE AND MERRY LADIES OF FRANCE AWAIT ME!

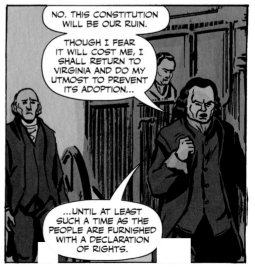

NO. THIS CONSTITUTION WILL BE OUR RUIN.

THOUGH I FEAR IT WILL COST ME, I SHALL RETURN TO VIRGINIA AND DO MY UTMOST TO PREVENT ITS ADOPTION...

...UNTIL AT LEAST SUCH A TIME AS THE PEOPLE ARE FURNISHED WITH A DECLARATION OF RIGHTS.

RATIFICATION: Federalists vs. Anti-Federalists

IN THE VOTE TO SEND DELEGATES TO RATIFY THE CONSTITUTION, MORE PEOPLE WOULD HAVE A SAY ON THEIR LAWS—AND THE SHAPE OF THEIR FUTURE—THAN EVER BEFORE.

AND FOR THIS VOTE, MOST STATES REDUCED OR ABOLISHED THEIR RULES ABOUT OWNING PROPERTY.

UP TO THAT TIME A *FEDERALIST* WAS SOMEONE WHO BELIEVED FIRST AND FOREMOST IN THE SOVEREIGNTY OF THE STATES, WHILE AN *ANTI-FEDERALIST* WANTED A STRONG, CENTRAL GOVERNMENT TO RULE OVER THEM, JUST AS THE CONSTITUTION WOULD ESTABLISH...

...BUT IN WHAT TODAY WOULD BE CALLED POLITICAL SPIN, THE ONES PUSHING HARDEST TO RATIFY THE CONSTITUTION TOOK THE FEDERALIST NAME FOR THEIR OWN PURPOSE, TO HELP WIN OVER THE COMMON PEOPLE.

UNDER THE PEN NAME PUBLIUS, HAMILTON, MADISON, AND JOHN JAY WROTE 85 ESSAYS NOW KNOWN AS *THE FEDERALIST PAPERS* TO EXPLAIN AND CHAMPION THEIR CAUSE.

To the people of the state of New York: you are called upon to deliberate on a new Constitution for the United States of America ...

NOW STUCK WITH THE ANTI-FEDERALIST NAME, OPPONENTS OF RATIFICATION—MANY PEOPLE, MANY DIFFERENT IDEAS—ATTACKED!

SOME THOUGHT THE CONSTITUTION, WHICH NEVER MENTIONS GOD, WAS ANTIRELIGIOUS.

WITH NO RELIGIOUS TEST FOR OFFICE, PAGANS, DEISTS, AND MAHOMETANS MIGHT OBTAIN OFFICE!

MANY RESENTED THAT THE FRAMERS HAD OVERSTEPPED THEIR JOB OF SIMPLY FIXING THE ARTICLES OF CONFEDERATION...

...WHAT RIGHT HAD THEY TO SAY, WE, THE PEOPLE...WHO AUTHORIZED THEM TO SPEAK THE LANGUAGE OF WE, THE PEOPLE, INSTEAD OF WE, THE STATES?

THE GREATNESS OF THE POWERS GIVEN... PRODUCE A COALITION OF MONARCHY MEN, MILITARY MEN, ARISTOCRATS AND DRONES. WHOSE NOISE, IMPUDENCE AND ZEAL EXCEEDS ALL BELIEF!

...AND HAD SET UP A POWERFUL NEW GOVERNMENT TO DOMINATE THE STATES.

THEY WERE SUSPICIOUS OF ALL POLITICAL POWER AND WANTED TO KEEP AMERICA A COUNTRY OF LANDOWNING FARMERS FOREVER.

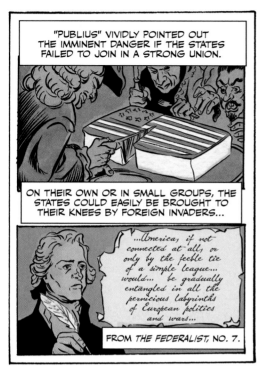

"PUBLIUS" VIVIDLY POINTED OUT THE IMMINENT DANGER IF THE STATES FAILED TO JOIN IN A STRONG UNION.

ON THEIR OWN OR IN SMALL GROUPS, THE STATES COULD EASILY BE BROUGHT TO THEIR KNEES BY FOREIGN INVADERS...

...America, if not connected at all, or only by the feeble tie of a simple league... would... be gradually entangled in all the pernicious labyrinths of European politics and wars...

FROM *THE FEDERALIST*, NO. 7.

...OR, GIVEN ALL THE FIERCE COMPETITION BETWEEN THEM, BY EACH OTHER.

OVER TIME BLOODSHED BETWEEN THEM COULD BECOME AS COMMON AS AMONG EUROPE'S MANY COUNTRIES IN THEIR CENTURIES OF ARMED CONFLICTS.

...we shall be... an infinity of little jealous, clashing, tumultuous commonwealths, the wretched nurseries of unceasing discord...

FROM *THE FEDERALIST*, NO 9.

AND JUST AS IMPORTANT, "PUBLIUS" SET FORTH WHY THE STATES SHOULD FORM A UNION.

ONE PIVOTAL REASON...

THAT'S RIGHT, MEN! KEEP AT IT!

AS LONG AS YOU DO IT ALL TOGETHER—IN A UNION—THE MORE YOU PULL, THE MORE STABLE WE WILL ALL BE!

...THAT THE BIGGER THE COUNTRY—THE MORE DIVERSE ITS PEOPLE, THEIR PASSIONS AND IDEAS ABOUT WHAT THEY WANT FROM GOVERNMENT—THE BETTER.

FROM *THE FEDERALIST*, NO. 10: "THE SMALLER THE SOCIETY... THE FEWER THE DISTINCT PARTIES AND INTERESTS, THE MORE FREQUENTLY WILL A MAJORITY...EXECUTE...PLANS OF OPPRESSION. EXTEND THE SPHERE...TAKE IN A GREATER VARIETY OF PARTIES AND INTERESTS; YOU MAKE IT LESS PROBABLE THAT A MAJORITY... [WILL] INVADE THE RIGHTS OF OTHER CITIZENS..."

NINE MONTHS AFTER THE CONSTITUTION WAS SIGNED, DEBATE STILL RAGED...

...AND ONLY EIGHT STATES HAD RATIFIED THE DOCUMENT.

IT WAS NOT YET LAW.

IN MASSACHUSETTS THE DEBATE WAS PARTICULARLY BITTER, AND THE VOTE CLOSE.

ITS CONSENT CAME ONLY WITH A LIST OF CHANGES ITS PEOPLE WANTED.

AND THE STATES OF VIRGINIA AND NEW YORK WERE STILL HOLDING OUT. THERE COULD BE NO LASTING UNION WITHOUT THEM.

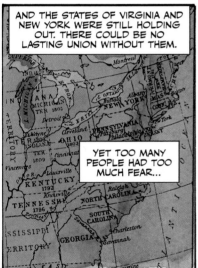

YET TOO MANY PEOPLE HAD TOO MUCH FEAR...

...THAT THE GOVERNMENT WOULD SIMPLY BE TOO POWERFUL.

WITH THREATS OF A NEW CONVENTION BEING CALLED, FEDERALISTS WON THEIR LINCHPIN NINTH STATE...

...AND NEW YORK AND VIRGINIA, BUT ONLY BY PROMISING TO QUICKLY ADD ONE THING TO THE CONSTITUTION...

...SOMETHING ECHOED IN THE WORDS OF FUTURE PRESIDENT THOMAS JEFFERSON.

A Bill of Rights is what the people are entitled to against every Government On earth, general or particular, and what no just Government should refuse...

The Bill of Rights: AMENDMENTS 1–10

THE POWER OF A GOVERNMENT CAN BE ENORMOUS. IF LEFT UNCHECKED, DANGEROUS.

ARTICLES I-VII OF THE CONSTITUTION MOSTLY GIVE GOVERNMENT POWER. BUT WITH THE BILL OF RIGHTS...

...PROPOSED BY THE FIRST CONGRESS, DRAFTED BY MADISON, AND SWIFTLY RATIFIED IN 1791...

...GOVERNMENT VOLUNTARILY GIVES UP POWER. IT RESTRAINS ITSELF.

AFTER ALL, ONE OF THE CORNERSTONE IDEAS OF THE AMERICAN REVOLUTION ITSELF IS THAT PEOPLE HAVE CERTAIN RIGHTS *BY BIRTH*.

AND SO THE BILL OF RIGHTS CONFIRMS THIS. THUS, THE CONSTITUTION REASSERTS THAT IT IS THE PEOPLE – NOT THEIR GOVERNMENT – WHO RULE.

THE RIGHT TO TRIAL BY JURY?

THANKS... I ALREADY HAVE ONE.

THE BILL OF RIGHTS SPELLS OUT WHAT FREEDOMS THE GOVERNMENT MAY NOT TAKE AWAY. IT IS THERE TO PROTECT YOUR RIGHTS, NOT TO GIVE THEM TO YOU.

TODAY MOST THINK ABOUT THE BILL OF RIGHTS AS EXCLUSIVELY PROTECTING THE RIGHTS OF THE INDIVIDUAL AGAINST THE MAJORITY.

BUT THE ANTI-FEDERALISTS WERE EQUALLY CONCERNED ABOUT PROTECTING THE MAJORITY.

...THAT IS, THE PEOPLE, OR GROUPS OF PEOPLE—FROM GOVERNMENT.

FROM *THE FEDERALIST, NO. 51*: "IT IS OF GREAT IMPORTANCE IN A REPUBLIC...TO GUARD THE SOCIETY AGAINST THE OPPRESSION OF ITS RULERS."

The First Amendment

THE FIRST AMENDMENT'S PROTECTIONS MAY BE THE BEST-KNOWN IN THE ENTIRE BILL OF RIGHTS.

THEY CONCERN *RELIGION*, *SPEECH*, THE *PRESS*, *ASSEMBLY*, AND *PETITION*.

I WANT YOU TO VOTE!

TO PARTICIPATE MEANINGFULLY IN GOVERNMENT—TO VOTE, SERVE ON JURIES, OR RUN FOR OFFICE—PEOPLE MUST BE FREE TO PURSUE A WIDE SPECTRUM OF FACTS AND OPINION.

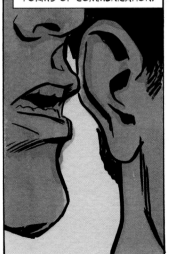

SO THE FIRST AMENDMENT PROTECTS OUR LIBERTY BOTH TO EXPRESS AND BE EXPOSED TO IDEAS AND OPINIONS—ESPECIALLY UNPOPULAR ONES. IT COVERS ALL FORMS OF COMMUNICATION.

BUT AS RECENTLY AS 1940, IN AN 8-1 DECISION, THE SUPREME COURT RULED THAT SCHOOLS COULD FORCE CHILDREN TO RECITE THE PLEDGE OF ALLEGIANCE. EVEN IF THEIR RELIGION DID NOT PERMIT IT!

JEHOVAH'S WITNESSES CHILDREN WILLIAM AND LILLIAN GOBITIS, EXPELLED FROM SCHOOL FOR REFUSING TO SALUTE THE FLAG.

THIS FACT, AND THAT THE DECISION IN *MINERSVILLE SCHOOL DISTRICT V. GOBITIS* (1940) WAS QUICKLY OVERRULED, POINTS OUT TWO THINGS. FIRST, THAT...

WE ARE UNDER A CONSTITUTION, BUT THE CONSTITUTION IS WHAT THE JUDGES SAY IT IS...

CHARLES EVAN HUGHES, CHIEF JUSTICE OF THE UNITED STATES, 1930-1941.

...THE SUPREME COURT, MANY TIMES IN ITS HISTORY, HAS COMPLETELY REVERSED ITS OWN RULINGS.

SECOND, THAT FREEDOM OF SPEECH AND THE PRESS HAS COME A LONG WAY.

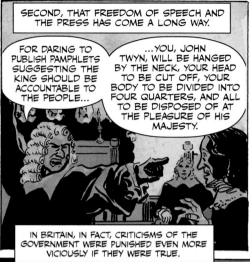

FOR DARING TO PUBLISH PAMPHLETS SUGGESTING THE KING SHOULD BE ACCOUNTABLE TO THE PEOPLE...

...YOU, JOHN TWYN, WILL BE HANGED BY THE NECK, YOUR HEAD TO BE CUT OFF, YOUR BODY TO BE DIVIDED INTO FOUR QUARTERS, AND ALL TO BE DISPOSED OF AT THE PLEASURE OF HIS MAJESTY.

IN BRITAIN, IN FACT, CRITICISMS OF THE GOVERNMENT WERE PUNISHED EVEN MORE VICIOUSLY IF THEY WERE TRUE.

THE FIRST AMENDMENT IS NOT *ABSOLUTE.* IF AN INDIVIDUAL'S SPEECH VIOLATES THE RIGHTS OF OTHERS, IT MAY NOT BE PROTECTED.

ZONE OF FREEDOM...

UNPROTECTED ZONE

FIST

NOSE

(FIST MAY MOVE AT WILL.)

(FIST MAY NOT ENTER AT HIGH VELOCITY.)

AS JUSTICE OLIVER WENDELL HOLMES SAID, "THE RIGHT TO SWING MY FIST ENDS WHERE THE OTHER MAN'S NOSE BEGINS."

GOVERNMENT MAY PUT REASONABLE RESTRICTIONS ON CERTAIN "CLASSES" OF SPEECH, LIKE...

...*INFLAMMATORY SPEECH,* MEANT TO SET OFF UNLAWFUL OR VIOLENT ACTS. IN *BRANDENBURG V. OHIO* (1969) IT WAS DECIDED THAT A SPEAKER MUST INTEND TO INCITE SUCH ACTS, AND THE SPEECH BE ACTUALLY LIKELY TO PRODUCE SUCH ACTS, TO BE OUTSIDE THE FIRST AMENDMENT.

...*DEFAMATORY SPEECH,* FALSE AND MALICIOUS SPEECH MEANT TO HARM A PERSON'S REPUTATION. THIS CAN BE VERY DIFFICULT TO PROVE IN THE CASES OF PUBLIC FIGURES LIKE POLITICIANS AND CELEBRITIES.

GOVERNMENT SCIENTIST IS SPY FOR CHINA

THERE GOES A WHITE BOY. GO GET HIM!

...*HATE SPEECH,* NOT SIMPLY THE EXPRESSION OF BIAS AGAINST AN INDIVIDUAL OR GROUP BUT ALSO SPEECH THAT IS LIKELY TO INFLICT EMOTIONAL HARM *AND* PROVOKE CRIMINAL ACTS.

...*TRUE THREATS,* SPEECH THAT A REASONABLE PERSON WOULD BELIEVE IS A SERIOUS EXPRESSION OF INTENT TO INFLICT HARM.

IF YOU TESTIFY AGAINST HIM IN COURT TOMORROW YOU'RE *DEAD.*

COPYRIGHTED SPEECH FALSE ADVERTISING INDECENCY, OBSCENITY AND *PORNOGRAPHY,* TO BEAR FIRST AMENDMENT SCRUTINY.

A CRITICAL THING TO REMEMBER ABOUT FREEDOM OF SPEECH AND THE PRESS: THE CONSTITUTION SAFEGUARDS ONLY AGAINST CENSORSHIP BY THE GOVERNMENT.

NEWS

IT IS NOT, SAY, A VIOLATION OF THE FIRST AMENDMENT FOR A NEWSPAPER TO REFUSE TO PUBLISH A REPORTER'S ARTICLE OR A RADIO STATION TO FIRE ITS ON-AIR TALENT.

FOR ANOTHER THING TO KEEP IN MIND ABOUT MANY BILL OF RIGHTS PROTECTIONS, IT IS NECESSARY TO LOOK INTO THE FUTURE.

UNTIL THE PASSAGE OF THE 14TH AMENDMENT 77 YEARS LATER...

...THE BILL OF RIGHTS APPLIED ONLY TO THE FEDERAL GOVERNMENT, NOT THE STATE GOVERNMENTS.

THE TEXT ITSELF SAYS EXPLICITLY: "CONGRESS SHALL MAKE NO LAW..." SO STATES WERE FREE TO MAKE LAWS POTENTIALLY VIOLATING ALL SORTS OF RIGHTS THE U.S. CONSTITUTION PROTECTS. AND EVEN THE 14TH AMENDMENT WENT LARGELY UNENFORCED FOR DECADES. IT TOOK MANY SUPREME COURT DECISIONS, AND BRAVE INDIVIDUALS STANDING UP FOR THEIR RIGHTS, TO *"INCORPORATE"* THE PROTECTIONS AT THE LEVELS OF GOVERNMENT MOST LIKELY TO IMPACT ON A CITIZEN'S LIFE.

FOR EXAMPLE, IN THE 1830S THE ABOLITIONIST REVEREND ELIJAH LOVEJOY PRINTED AN ANTISLAVERY NEWSPAPER ON THE WILD MISSOURI FRONTIER. THE FIRST AMENDMENT WAS NO HELP TO HIM.

LOVEJOY WAS MURDERED AND HIS PRINTING PLANT BURNED EVEN AFTER HE HAD RELOCATED TO ILLINOIS.

SUPREME COURT DECISIONS WERE TO PUT OUT OF PRACTICE A CALIFORNIA LAW AGAINST DISPLAYING THE COMMUNIST FLAG AND A TEXAS LAW AGAINST BURNING THE AMERICAN FLAG.

THESE ARE EXAMPLES OF PROTECTED *SYMBOLIC SPEECH*. *POLITICAL SPEECH* AFFORDS THE HIGHEST PROTECTION.

IS FREEDOM OF SPEECH AND THE PRESS A WEAKNESS, SINCE IT ALLOWS A FREE FLOW OF IDEAS THAT MIGHT UNDERMINE THE GOVERNMENT OR POPULAR NOTIONS OF MORALITY? OR IS IT A STRENGTH THAT ALLOWS ROBUST AND OPEN DEBATE SO THAT ALL IDEAS GET TO COMPETE AND THE BEST WIN OUT? DO WE TRUST THE GOVERNMENT, OR OURSELVES, TO DECIDE WHAT IDEAS ARE DANGEROUS? OR BAD? THE DEBATE CONTINUES...AND CHALLENGES TO THIS FIRST AMENDMENT PROTECTION CONTINUE TO SHAPE THE CHARACTER OF THE UNITED STATES.

LOOK CLOSELY AT THE FOLLOWING PHRASE FROM THE FIRST AMENDMENT:

"CONGRESS SHALL MAKE NO LAW RESPECTING AN ESTABLISHMENT OF RELIGION..."

IT GUARANTEES THAT AMERICANS HAVE FREEDOM OF RELIGION AND THAT THERE CAN NEVER BE AN OFFICIAL RELIGION FOR THE COUNTRY AS A WHOLE.

AFTER ALL, MANY EARLY IMMIGRANTS TO AMERICA LEFT ENGLAND BECAUSE THEIR WAYS OF WORSHIP CONFLICTED WITH THE OFFICIAL *CHURCH OF ENGLAND*.

BUT IN THE FRAMERS' TIME A FEW STATES HAD OFFICIAL CHURCHES. CONGRESS WAS NOT ALLOWED TO ALTER THAT! IT COULD MAKE NO LAW RESPECTING THEIR ALREADY ESTABLISHED RELIGIONS.

UNTIL 1818 CONNECTICUT RECOGNIZED AN OFFICIAL CONGREGATIONALIST CHURCH.

1868 THE 14th AMENDMENT

ALL STATES VOLUNTARILY GAVE UP THEIR STATE CHURCHES BEFORE THE CIVIL WAR. REGARDLESS, THE 14TH AMENDMENT WOULD MAKE OFFICIAL STATE CHURCHES ILLEGAL TODAY.

AGAIN, FREEDOM OF RELIGION PROTECTIONS ARE NOT ABSOLUTE. IN *REYNOLDS V. U.S.* (1879) THE SUPREME COURT FOUND THE MORMON CHURCH'S PRACTICE OF POLYGAMY ILLEGAL.

ONE IS ALSO FREE TO HAVE NO RELIGION. *WELSH V. U.S.* (1970) ESTABLISHED THAT PEOPLE WITH DEEP MORAL OR ETHICAL ANTIWAR BELIEFS CAN HAVE *CONSCIENTIOUS OBJECTOR* EXEMPTION FROM MILITARY COMBAT.

THE *FREEDOM OF CONSCIENCE* IDEALS THE REVOLUTIONARY GENERATION STROVE FOR ALSO EXTEND TO *FREEDOM OF ASSOCIATION*, MEANING THAT GOVERNMENT HAS NO BUSINESS KNOWING WHAT COMPANY YOU MIX WITH OR WHICH ORGANIZATIONS YOU BELONG TO. OR FORCING YOU TO ASSOCIATE WITH PEOPLE OR ORGANIZATIONS.

IN *NAACP V. ALABAMA* (1958) THE SUPREME COURT HELD THAT A PROMINENT CIVIL RIGHTS ORGANIZATION DID NOT HAVE TO HAND OVER A LIST OF ITS MEMBERS' NAMES AND ADDRESSES TO THE STATE GOVERNMENT.

BUT *FREEDOM OF ASSEMBLY* IS BIGGER THAN A SIMPLE RIGHT FOR GROUPS OF LIKE-MINDED INDIVIDUALS, POLITICAL PARTIES, OR INTEREST GROUPS TO COME TOGETHER IN THE NAME OF INFLUENCING PUBLIC POLICY.

IT ALSO MEANS "WE, THE PEOPLE" HAVE A RIGHT TO MEET PEACEFULLY IN CONVENTION AND ALTER OR ABOLISH GOVERNMENT IF IT FAILS TO REPRESENT US.

REMEMBER, "WE, THE PEOPLE" FORMED THE UNION. CONSIDER THESE WORDS FROM THE DECLARATION OF INDEPENDENCE: "...THAT WHENEVER ANY FORM OF GOVERNMENT BECOMES DESTRUCTIVE OF THESE ENDS, IT IS THE RIGHT OF THE PEOPLE TO ALTER OR TO ABOLISH IT, AND TO INSTITUTE NEW GOVERNMENT... AS TO THEM SHALL SEEM MOST LIKELY TO EFFECT THEIR SAFETY AND HAPPINESS." BUT *ALL* THE PEOPLE PEACEFULLY MEETING IN CONVENTION AND *SOME* OF THE PEOPLE CHOOSING TO TAKE UP ARMS AGAINST AND BREAK AWAY FROM THE UNION ARE TWO VERY DIFFERENT THINGS.

the 2nd AMENDMENT

THE SECOND AMENDMENT—ONE THAT OFTEN SPARKS CONTROVERSY—ACTUALLY DEALS WITH TWO SEPARATE IDEAS...

...THE MILITIA AND...

...THE RIGHT TO BEAR ARMS.

AS WE HAVE SEEN, BEFORE THERE WERE POLICE FORCES OR A MILITARY...

...THE MILITIA WAS AN INSTITUTION IN SOCIETY. ITS MEMBERS ORGANIZED TO PROTECT THEIR FARMS AND TOWNS. THEY WERE NOT VIGILANTES.

THEY WERE ARMED CIVILIANS WITH VESTED INTERESTS IN THEIR COMMUNITIES.

WHAT AMERICANS (AND BRITISH SUBJECTS BEFORE THEM) DISTRUSTED MOST WERE *MERCENARIES*, GUNS FOR HIRE WITH NO COMMUNITY TIES AND *NO* LOYALTY TO ANYONE BUT THOSE WHO PAID THEM.

THEY DID NOT REPRESENT THE PEOPLE.

TO ANTI-FEDERALISTS, AN ARMED PEOPLE WERE A CHECK ON GOVERNMENT POWER. THEY SOUGHT ASSURANCES THE GOVERNMENT WOULD NOT PUT A MERCENARY FORCE BETWEEN ITSELF AND THE PEOPLE...

...OR TAKE AWAY THEIR WEAPONS IF IT DID.

Article the fourth... A well regulated militia, being necessary to the security of a free state the right of the people to keep and bear arms shall not be infringed.

THE SECOND AMENDMENT DELIVERED ON BOTH COUNTS. WITH ITS OPENING CLAUSE, IT CERTIFIES THAT THE MILITIA IS LEGITIMATE. IT GOES ON TO CONFIRM THAT THE PEOPLE RETAIN THE RIGHT TO POSSESS AND USE FIREARMS FOR SELF-DEFENSE, FOR HUNTING GAME, FOR SPORT, AND AS A BULWARK AGAINST TYRANNY.

IN THE MILITIA'S HEYDAY, GUNS WERE A CRUCIAL PART OF DAILY LIFE. SOME STATES HAD LAWS REQUIRING MEN TO OWN GUNS. VIRTUALLY ALL THE FRAMERS OWNED THEM. MILITIAMEN HAD FOUGHT IN THE REVOLUTION, AND THE 1792 U.S. MILITIA ACT OBLIGATED MEN 18-45 TO ENROLL IN THEIR LOCAL MILITIAS.

STILL, THERE WERE ALWAYS LAWS REGULATING THE USE OF FIREARMS—FOR EXAMPLE, ORDINANCES AGAINST SHOOTING THEM NEAR BARNS OR BUILDINGS.

IF FIRST AMENDMENT RIGHTS ARE NOT ABSOLUTE, SHOULD THE SECOND AMENDMENT RIGHT TO "KEEP AND BEAR ARMS" BE?

AND COULD MEN IN THE LATE 1700S HAVE EVEN IMAGINED THE POWER OF THE "ARMS" AVAILABLE TODAY?

THOSE WHO SAY THAT THE SECOND AMENDMENT GUARANTEES AN UNLIMITED RIGHT TO OWN AND USE GUNS OVERLOOK...

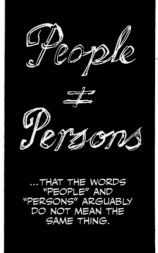

People ≠ Persons

...THAT THE WORDS "PEOPLE" AND "PERSONS" ARGUABLY DO NOT MEAN THE SAME THING.

IN THE 18TH-CENTURY LANGUAGE OF THE CONSTITUTION AND ITS FIRST TEN AMENDMENTS, "PERSONS" ARE EVERYONE, EVEN SLAVES.

"PEOPLE" ARE THOSE WHO QUALIFY FOR *POLITICAL RIGHTS:* TO VOTE, HOLD PUBLIC OFFICE, SERVE ON JURIES AND IN THE MILITIA.

NO LEGAL RACE- OR GENDER-BASED SECOND CLASS EXISTS TODAY. STILL, SOME "PERSONS" CANNOT VOTE OR SERVE ON JURIES: CHILDREN, THE MENTALLY ILL, AND, IN MOST STATES, *FELONS* IN PRISON, ON PROBATION, OR ON PAROLE.

SO, IF "PEOPLE" HAVE THE RIGHT TO BEAR ARMS, GOVERNMENT HAS THE POWER TO IMPOSE FAIR QUALIFICATIONS ON THAT RIGHT.

AMONG THESE QUALIFICATIONS, *DISTRICT OF COLUMBIA V. HELLER* (2008) SPECIFIED THAT THE TYPES OF ARMS THE SECOND AMENDMENT PROTECTS ARE THOSE "TYPICALLY POSSESSED BY LAW-ABIDING CITIZENS FOR LAWFUL PURPOSES."

IT ALSO LET STAND THE PRACTICE OF KEEPING GUNS OUT OF THE HANDS OF FELONS AND THE MENTALLY ILL, AND REQUIRING FIREARMS TO BE REGISTERED AND LICENSED.

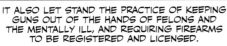

AFTER DECADES OF AMBIGUITY, THE *HELLER* DECISION FINALLY CONFIRMED THAT THE RIGHT TO BEAR ARMS DOES NOT FALL EXCLUSIVELY TO THOSE IN THE NATIONAL GUARD OR LAW ENFORCEMENT.

YET FEW AMERICANS WOULD DISAVOW THE PROBLEMS OF VIOLENT CRIMES AND HARMFUL ACCIDENTS INVOLVING GUNS.

THE CLASH OF INTERESTS OVER GUN CONTROL CONTINUES TO FUEL DEBATE. BUT THE FATE OF THE SECOND AMENDMENT ULTIMATELY FALLS TO THE PEOPLE-NOT THE COURTS.

The Third Amendment

IN 1757...

NEARLY TWO DECADES BEFORE THE AMERICAN REVOLUTION...

...BRITAIN AND FRANCE BOTH CLAIMED, AND WERE FIGHTING OVER, A VAST, INLAND TRACT OF NORTH AMERICA CALLED THE OHIO COUNTRY...

...IN A CONFLICT NOW CALLED THE FRENCH AND INDIAN WAR.

K-THOOM

CRACK CRACK

WITH FEW SHELTERS IN THIS WILDERNESS, BRITISH SOLDIERS WERE ACCOMMODATED, OR QUARTERED, IN THE PRIVATE HOMES OF SETTLERS.

WITH FRANCE DEFEATED, THE SOLDIERS RETURNED TO THE AMERICAN COLONIES...

...WHERE PATRIOTS WERE BECOMING EVER MORE WARY OF BRITISH RULE.

ANGRY COLONISTS RESENTED THE BRITISH PARLIAMENT'S TWO *QUARTERING ACTS*, KEEPING SOLDIERS IN THEIR MIDST AND FORCING THEM TO PROVIDE THEM WITH DRINK AND ARTICLES LIKE CANDLES, SALT, AND EATING UTENSILS.

THE THIRD AMENDMENT—BLOCKING THE GOVERNMENT FROM QUARTERING TROOPS IN PRIVATE HOMES—IS A LEGACY OF THIS BITTERNESS.

THE THIRD AMENDMENT MIGHT SEEM LIKE AN ODDITY LEFT OVER FROM HISTORY.

TIME CAPSULE

WHAT IS IT?

BUT TOGETHER WITH THE SECOND AMENDMENT'S EMPHASIS ON A CITIZEN MILITIA...

...IT UPHOLDS, IN PEACETIME, THE SUPREMACY OF CIVILIAN LIFE AND VALUES OVER THE MILITARY...

...AS WELL AS A PROTECTION OF *PRIVACY RIGHTS* AND *PROPERTY RIGHTS* FROM GOVERNMENT INTRUSION.

DO NOT DISTURB

The Fourth Amendment

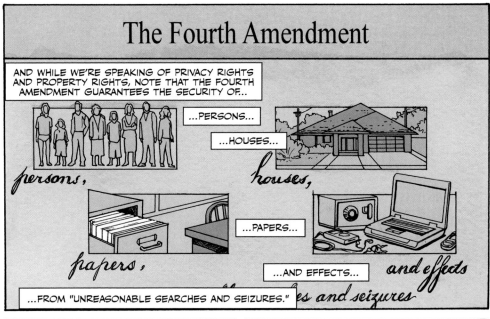

AND WHILE WE'RE SPEAKING OF PRIVACY RIGHTS AND PROPERTY RIGHTS, NOTE THAT THE FOURTH AMENDMENT GUARANTEES THE SECURITY OF...

...PERSONS...

persons,

...HOUSES...

houses,

...PAPERS...

papers,

...AND EFFECTS...

and effects

...FROM "UNREASONABLE SEARCHES AND SEIZURES."

es and seizures

WHAT DOES THIS BOIL DOWN TO?

FOR ONE THING, POLICE OR FEDERAL AGENTS DO NOT HAVE THE POWER TO ARREST ANYONE THEY WANT, AT WILL...

...NOR, EVEN IN INVESTIGATING A CRIME, SIMPLY TO ENTER AND SEARCH A PRIVATE PLACE AND SEIZE EVIDENCE.

THE FOURTH AMENDMENT HAS ITS ROOTS IN BRITAIN'S TRYING TO KEEP AMERICA FROM BUILDING ITS OWN SHIPS, CONDUCTING ITS OWN TRADE.

WITH *WRITS OF ASSISTANCE*, THE KING'S OFFICERS COULD ENTER ANY PLACE, ANYTIME, TO SEARCH FOR CONTRABAND GOODS.

AMERICANS DID NOT WANT THEIR GOVERNMENT TO HAVE THIS POWER.

GENERALLY, MAKING ARRESTS OR TAKING EVIDENCE REQUIRES *PROBABLE CAUSE*, "REASONABLE SUSPICION" OF A CRIME.

ONCE PROBABLE CAUSE IS ESTABLISHED, A COURT MUST ISSUE A *WARRANT* TO AUTHORIZE AN ARREST OR SEARCH.

WARRANTS MUST CLEARLY DESCRIBE THE PLACE TO BE SEARCHED OR THE PEOPLE OR THINGS TO BE SEIZED.

REMEMBER, THE FOURTH AMENDMENT PROTECTS ONLY AGAINST *UNREASONABLE* SEARCHES AND SEIZURES.

MORE ARRESTS ARE MADE *WITHOUT* WARRANTS THAN *WITH*...

...IN A WHOLE CLASS OF CIRCUMSTANCES THAT, ON THEIR OWN, AMOUNT TO *PROBABLE CAUSE*.

FOR EXAMPLE, IF CRIMES ARE CONDUCTED AND/OR CRIMINAL EVIDENCE IS FOUND "IN PLAIN VIEW," SEIZURES ARE NOT "UNREASONABLE."

"PLAIN VIEW" ALSO APPLIES TO WHAT CAN BE SEEN ON PRIVATE PROPERTY FROM THE AIR.

THOUGH MANY SUPREME COURT CASES HAVE NARROWED WHAT IS AND ISN'T PROBABLE CAUSE...

PROBABLE!

IMPROBABLE!

PROBABLE!

IMPROBABLE!

PROBABLE!

IMPROBABLE!

...THE CIRCUMSTANCES OF COUNTLESS ARRESTS AND SEIZURES ARE EVALUATED IN COURT EVERY DAY. *BOYD V. U.S.* (1886) ESTABLISHED THAT THE FOURTH AMENDMENT PROTECTS PEOPLE FROM BEING FORCED TO FURNISH EVIDENCE AGAINST THEMSELVES.

HMM... YES. HMM...

INVOICE

...WE HAVE BEEN UP TO NO GOOD, HAVEN'T WE, MR. BOYD?

WHAT HAPPENS WHEN EVIDENCE OF A CRIME IS ILLEGALLY SEIZED...

...WITHOUT A WARRANT IN CIRCUMSTANCES THAT MERIT ONE?

THE ASSUMPTION HAD LONG BEEN THAT IT COULD STILL BE USED IN COURT...

...THAT IS, UNTIL *WEEKS V. U.S.* (1914), THE CASE OF A MAN APPEALING HIS CONVICTION ON HELPING RUN AN ILLEGAL LOTTERY THROUGH THE MAILS, A FEDERAL CRIME.

IF LETTERS AND PRIVATE DOCUMENTS CAN THUS BE SEIZED AND HELD AND USED IN EVIDENCE...THE PROTECTION OF THE FOURTH AMENDMENT...IS OF NO VALUE AND...MIGHT AS WELL BE STRICKEN FROM THE CONSTITUTION.

THE EFFORTS OF THE COURTS... ARE NOT TO BE AIDED BY THE SACRIFICE OF THOSE GREAT PRINCIPLES ESTABLISHED BY YEARS OF ENDEAVOR AND SUFFERING...

BECAUSE THE MARSHAL IN *WEEKS* DID NOT HAVE A WARRANT WHEN COLLECTING EVIDENCE, WEEKS'S CONVICTION WAS REVERSED.

THIS CASE IS CREDITED FOR BEGINNING *THE EXCLUSIONARY RULE,* MEANING THAT FROM THEN ON, EVIDENCE TAKEN IN VIOLATION OF THE FOURTH AMENDMENT CANNOT BE USED IN A CRIMINAL TRIAL. THAT EVIDENCE IS INADMISSIBLE.

THE CONSEQUENCES OF THIS ARE CLEAR TO SEE; SOMETIMES IT LETS THE GUILTY WALK FREE. BUT THE IDEA BEHIND THE EXCLUSIONARY RULE IS TO INSURE THAT LAW ENFORCEMENT AGENCIES DO THEIR JOBS CORRECTLY. IT IS TO DETER OFFICIAL MISCONDUCT.

THERE ARE, HOWEVER, LIMITED CASES IN WHICH THE EXCLUSIONARY RULE DOES NOT APPLY.

WITH THE FOURTH AMENDMENT...

...IT IS EASY TO SEE HOW INTERPRETATION OF THE CONSTITUTION CAN CHANGE WITH THE TIMES.

IN *OLMSTEAD V. U.S.* (1928) GOVERNMENT AGENTS HELPED CONVICT CRIMINALS BY ELECTRONICALLY EAVESDROPPING ON THEIR TELEPHONE CONVERSATIONS, OR *WIRETAPPING.*

THE SUPREME COURT DECIDED THEIR EVIDENCE *WAS* ADMISSIBLE WITHOUT A WARRANT BECAUSE NO "PLACE" WAS ENTERED, OR "THING" SEIZED!

IN A NOTABLE *DISSENTING OPINION*— AN OFFICIAL DISAGREEMENT WITH THE MAJORITY RULING IN A CASE—JUSTICE LOUIS BRANDEIS WROTE:

...every unjustifiable intrusion by the Government upon the privacy of the individual, whatever the means employed, must be deemed a violation of the Fourth Amendment.

EVIDENCE ILLEGALLY GATHERED THROUGH WIRETAPPING WAS DETERMINED TO BE IN VIOLATION OF THE FOURTH AMENDMENT WITH *NARDONE V. U.S.* (1937).

BUT THE 2001 *USA PATRIOT ACT* EXPANDED GOVERNMENT POWER TO SEIZE RECORDS AND CONDUCT ELECTRONIC SURVEILLANCE WITHOUT WARRANTS OR PROBABLE CAUSE IN TERRORISM INVESTIGATIONS.

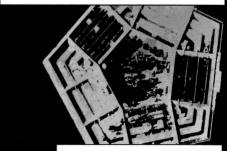

TO DATE THE ACT'S MANY PROVISIONS HAVE NOT RECEIVED A SUPREME COURT TEST.

STILL, SINCE *NARDONE*, PERSONAL COMMUNICATIONS ARE GENERALLY SEEN TO FALL UNDER FOURTH AMENDMENT PROTECTIONS.

THEN I CUT HIS CAR'S BRAKE LINES, THEN I TOOK A—

NOT HERE, YOU DUMB MAGGOT! WE'RE IN PUBLIC!

ANYTHING ANYONE HEARS YOU SAY IS *ADMISSIBLE* UNDER JUSTICE HARLAN'S CONCURRING OPINION IN *KATZ V. U.S.* (1967)...

...AT LEAST IN SITUATIONS IN WHICH ONE HAS A "REASONABLE EXPECTATION OF PRIVACY."

YOU MAY THINK YOU HAVE A "REASONABLE EXPECTATION OF PRIVACY" IN YOUR CAR.

BUT SINCE VEHICLES ARE, IN A WAY, MOVING TARGETS THAT RESIST HAVING WARRANTS APPLIED TO THEM...

PLEASE POP THE TRUNK, SIR.

...SEARCHES OF CARS, AND ANYTHING INSIDE THEM THAT A LAW ENFORCEMENT OFFICER REASONABLY BELIEVES MIGHT CONTAIN CRIMINAL EVIDENCE, ARE ALLOWABLE SINCE *CALIFORNIA V. ACEVEDO* (1991).

1868 THE 14th AMENDMENT

REMEMBER: THE BILL OF RIGHTS APPLIED ONLY TO THE FEDERAL GOVERNMENT UNTIL THE GRADUAL 14TH AMENDMENT INCORPORATION. THE 4TH AMENDMENT WAS APPLIED TO THE STATES FIRST IN PART WITH *WOLF V. COLORADO* (1949) AND FINALLY WITH *MAPP V. OHIO* (1961).

TK TK

CREAK

WHO—WHO
ARE YOU?

HEH-HEH. HE WANTS
TO KNOW WHO
WE ARE.

JOSEPH
K.?

WHAT? WHY?
ON WHAT
CHARGE?

THAT'S SOMETHING
WE'RE NOT ALLOWED TO
TELL YOU. "PROCEEDINGS"
ARE UNDER WAY.

YES...

YOU
ARE UNDER
ARREST.

WHAT'S GOING ON? WHO TOLD YOU I DID SOMETHING WRONG?

OH, NO ONE...

...BUT I'M SURE *YOU'LL* TELL US WHAT YOU DID. I'M SURE YOU'LL TELL US PLENTY.

IT WAS EXACTLY TO PREVENT SINISTER ABUSES OF POWER LIKE THIS THAT THE NEXT GROUP OF AMENDMENTS, BEGINNING WITH THE FIFTH, WERE DESIGNED.

AMERICANS DEMANDING A BILL OF RIGHTS WANTED PROTECTION FROM A GOVERNMENT THAT MIGHT HARASS THEM WITH MALICIOUS, UNFOUNDED, OR FALLACIOUS COURT TRIALS.

IF PROBABLE CAUSE WAS TO BE NECESSARY FOR ARREST OR SEARCH WARRANTS...

...THEN SOME KIND OF PROBABLE CAUSE SHOULD ALSO BE NECESSARY FOR TRIALS OF *CAPITAL CRIMES* (WHERE THE GUILTY FACES A DEATH SENTENCE) AND WHAT THE CONSTITUTION CALLS *INFAMOUS CRIMES* (WHERE THE GUILTY FACES PRISON SENTENCES LONGER THAN ONE YEAR).

THE *FEDERAL GRAND JURY* IS THE CONSTITUTION'S ANSWER TO THIS.

FEDERAL GRAND JURIES ARE MADE UP OF 16-23 CITIZENS. IN SECRET HEARINGS, *PROSECUTORS* PRESENT THEM WITH A COMPLAINT, OR *INDICTMENT*, AGAINST THE ACCUSED. THE GRAND JURY THEN HEARS EVIDENCE AND WITNESS TESTIMONY.

IF THE GRAND JURY DECIDES THERE IS ENOUGH EVIDENCE TO CONDUCT A TRIAL, THE INDICTMENT IS RETURNED. THE ACCUSED MAY BE ARRESTED, AND A TRIAL PROCEEDS.

THE CONSTITUTION EXEMPTS MEMBERS OF THE MILITARY FROM GRAND JURY PROTECTION. INSTEAD, THE *UNIFORM CODE OF MILITARY JUSTICE* APPLIES AS WELL AS TO MEMBERS OF THE MILITIA IN TIMES OF WAR OR "PUBLIC DANGER."

1868
THE 14th
AMENDMENT

THE SUPREME COURT HAS DETERMINED THAT THE GRAND JURY PROVISION DOES NOT APPLY AGAINST THE STATES (SOME OF WHICH HAVE THEIR OWN GRAND JURY SYSTEMS). THIS IS AMONG A FEW AMENDMENTS THAT RESIST INCORPORATION.

IN THE AMERICAN LEGAL SYSTEM THE ACCUSED DOES NOT HAVE TO PROVE INNOCENCE.

WELL, DEFENDANT... ...*ACCOUNT FOR YOURSELF!*

INSTEAD, THE BURDEN OF PROOF FOR GUILT IS ON THE PROSECUTION.

ON THE ADVICE OF COUNSEL, I RESPECTFULLY AND REGRETFULLY DECLINE TO ANSWER THE QUESTION BASED ON MY CONSTITUTIONAL RIGHTS.

SO PER THE FIFTH AMENDMENT NO ONE MAY BE FORCED TO TESTIFY AGAINST HIM- OR HERSELF.

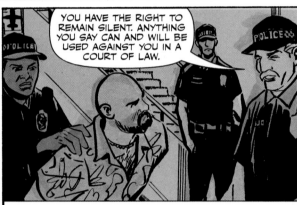

YOU HAVE THE RIGHT TO REMAIN SILENT. ANYTHING YOU SAY CAN AND WILL BE USED AGAINST YOU IN A COURT OF LAW.

THE SUPREME COURT CASE *MIRANDA V. ARIZONA* (1966) EXTENDS THE RIGHT AGAINST SELF-INCRIMINATION ALL THE WAY TO A SUSPECT'S INITIAL ARREST.

THE RIGHT TO REMAIN SILENT IS MEANT TO DISCOURAGE LAW ENFORCEMENT FROM FORCING CONFESSIONS BY TORTURE, THREAT OF TORTURE, OR OTHER FORMS OF PHYSICAL OR PSYCHOLOGICAL COERCION.

WE FIND THE DEFENDANT NOT GUILTY, YOUR HONOR.

THE FIFTH AMENDMENT DECLARES THAT ONCE *ACQUITTED*—FOUND NOT GUILTY BY A JURY—NO DEFENDANT MAY BE TRIED AGAIN FOR THE SAME CRIME. THERE CAN BE NO *DOUBLE JEOPARDY.*

THE *DUE PROCESS* GUARANTEE MEANS GOVERNMENT ACTION MUST NEVER BE IMPROPER OR UNFAIR. IT MUST STRICTLY FOLLOW RULES AND STEPS SET DOWN BY LAW.

WHAT? WHY? ON WHAT CHARGE?

THAT'S SOMETHING WE'RE NOT ALLOWED TO TELL YOU.

SO, FIRST, DUE PROCESS MUST BE *PROCEDURAL.* FOR EXAMPLE, THE ACCUSED HAS A RIGHT TO CLEAR CHARGES, AN IMPARTIAL JUDGE, AND THE OPPORTUNITY TO PRESENT A DEFENSE.

WHAT...?

THERE'S NOTHING IN THE EMPLOYEE HANDBOOK THAT SAYS I CAN'T TAKE A FIRE HOSE TO THE OFFICE WHEN I'M IN A BAD MOOD!

BUT STRICTLY FOLLOWING RULES DOES NOT ALWAYS ASSURE FAIRNESS AND JUSTICE.

SUBSTANTIVE DUE PROCESS MUST ALSO BE HEEDED. GOVERNMENT CANNOT JUST ACT FAIRLY. IT MUST ACTUALLY *BE* FAIR AND APPLY THE LAW EQUALLY TO ALL PEOPLE. IT CANNOT SINGLE OUT ANY PERSON OR GROUP FOR BETTER OR WORSE TREATMENT.

CONSIDER THIS: DOES YOUR RIGHT TO LIBERTY ALLOW YOU TO AGREE TO TAKE A JOB THAT DOES NOT PAY MINIMUM WAGE? AND WILL REQUIRE YOU TO PERFORM DANGEROUS WORK FOR LONG HOURS? UNDER UNSAFE CONDITIONS?

IN *LOCHNER V. NEW YORK* (1905) THE SUPREME COURT SAID THAT STATE LAW COULD NOT FORCE LIMITATIONS ON THE NUMBER OF HOURS A BAKERY OWNER COULD REQUIRE FROM HIS EMPLOYEES.

DECADES LATER *WEST COAST HOTEL V. PARRISH* (1937) TURNED THE TIDE AWAY FROM LOCHNER.

WEST COAST HOTEL

...LIBERTY...REQUIRES THE PROTECTION OF LAW AGAINST THE EVILS WHICH MENACE THE HEALTH, SAFETY, MORALS, AND WELFARE OF THE PEOPLE...REGULATION WHICH IS REASONABLE...

AND IS ADOPTED IN THE INTERESTS OF THE COMMUNITY IS DUE PROCESS.

IN OTHER WORDS, A LEVEL OF FAIR TREATMENT, FAIR WAGES, AND FAIR CONDITIONS FOR EVERYONE IS A HIGHER PRIORITY THAN ALLOWING PEOPLE TO MAKE CERTAIN HARMFUL DECISIONS FOR THEMSELVES.

BOTH STATE AND FEDERAL GOVERNMENTS ARE RECOGNIZED TO HAVE THE POWER OF *EMINENT DOMAIN*.

THAT MEANS THEY MAY TAKE PRIVATE PROPERTY FOR PUBLIC USE.

PROPERTY OF U.S. GOVT

THE FIFTH AMENDMENT AND ITS INCORPORATION AGAINST THE STATES GUARANTEE THAT WHEN DOING SO, STATES MUST COMPENSATE THE FORMER OWNERS IN A WAY THAT CONSTITUTES "A FULL AND PERFECT EQUIVALENT FOR THE PROPERTY TAKEN."

WHAT IS "PROPERTY" AND WHAT IS "PUBLIC USE" CAN STILL BE CONTROVERSIAL.

EMINENT DOMAIN

AS OF *KELO V. NEW LONDON* (2005), PRIVATE PROPERTY MAY BE TAKEN AND SOLD TO OTHER PRIVATE OWNERS IF THE USE IS DEEMED "OF GENERAL BENEFIT TO THE PUBLIC."

SHRAM

HOWEVER, IF GOVERNMENT DOES NOT ACTUALLY TAKE PROPERTY BUT BY ITS ACTION DIMINISHES HOW THE LAND CAN BE "USED" AND "ENJOYED,"* THAT, TOO, CAN HAVE FIFTH AMENDMENT CONSEQUENCES.

*U.S. V. CAUSBY (1946)

The Sixth Amendment

UNDER THE BRITISH MONARCHY, THE STRUGGLE FOR JUST TREATMENT UNDER THE LAW WAS SO GRUELING...

WE ARE THE BARONS, AND WE DEMAND CERTAIN RIGHTS AND LIBERTIES.

SIGN IT.

GRUMBLE GRUMBLE

SIGNING OF THE MAGNA CARTA, 1215.

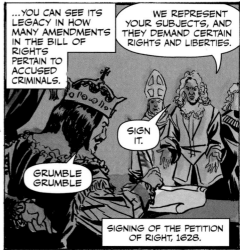

...YOU CAN SEE ITS LEGACY IN HOW MANY AMENDMENTS IN THE BILL OF RIGHTS PERTAIN TO ACCUSED CRIMINALS.

WE REPRESENT YOUR SUBJECTS, AND THEY DEMAND CERTAIN RIGHTS AND LIBERTIES.

SIGN IT.

GRUMBLE GRUMBLE

SIGNING OF THE PETITION OF RIGHT, 1628.

THE SIXTH AMENDMENT RIGHT TO A SPEEDY TRIAL PREVENTS THE PRESUMED INNOCENT FROM LANGUISHING IN JAIL.

American Justice
HOME OF SPEEDY SERVICE
DRIVE THRU
DRIVE

"SPEEDY" SETS NO SPECIFIC TIME FRAME. THE GOVERNMENT JUST MAY NOT SHOW MALICE OR UNFAIRNESS IN SETTING A TRIAL DATE.

MAY I TAKE YOUR ORDER, SIR?

YEAH. LEMME HAVE A PUBLIC TRIAL...

THIS PUBLIC-TRIAL RIGHT STEMS FROM THE PRACTICE OF OPPRESSIVE GOVERNMENTS CREATING FEAR BY MAKING THEIR TRIALS SECRET...

...AS CHARLES I HAD ABUSED THE POWER OF THE *STAR CHAMBER* COURT, AND THE CATHOLIC CHURCH THE POWER OF THE *SPANISH INQUISITION.*

ANOTHER REASON FOR THE RIGHT TO PUBLIC TRIALS? *AND* THE FACT THAT THERE IS A COMPULSORY *PROCESS* TO MAKE WITNESSES APPEAR IN COURT?

IT WAS THOUGHT PEOPLE ARE LESS LIKELY TO LIE BEFORE A JUDGE, A JURY, AND SPECTATORS.

...I'LL ALSO TAKE AN IMPARTIAL JURY...

AN IMPARTIAL JURY IS ESSENTIAL IN A CRIMINAL TRIAL. AFTER ALL, IF JURORS ARE PREDISPOSED TOWARD THE PROSECUTION OR THE DEFENSE, JUSTICE CANNOT PREVAIL.

WOULD YOU LIKE THAT IMPARTIAL JURY IN THE STATE AND DISTRICT WHERE THE ALLEGED CRIME WAS COMMITTED?

DEFINITELY.

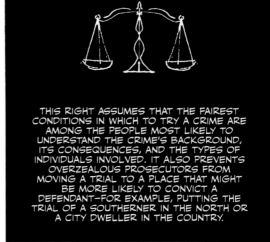

THIS RIGHT ASSUMES THAT THE FAIREST CONDITIONS IN WHICH TO TRY A CRIME ARE AMONG THE PEOPLE MOST LIKELY TO UNDERSTAND THE CRIME'S BACKGROUND, ITS CONSEQUENCES, AND THE TYPES OF INDIVIDUALS INVOLVED. IT ALSO PREVENTS OVERZEALOUS PROSECUTORS FROM MOVING A TRIAL TO A PLACE THAT MIGHT BE MORE LIKELY TO CONVICT A DEFENDANT—FOR EXAMPLE, PUTTING THE TRIAL OF A SOUTHERNER IN THE NORTH OR A CITY DWELLER IN THE COUNTRY.

YOU HAVE THE RIGHT TO HAVE AN ATTORNEY.

THE RIGHT TO COUNSEL—A LAWYER TO REPRESENT THE ACCUSED—EXTENDS EVEN TO BEING QUESTIONED AFTER AN ARREST IS MADE (*ESCOBEDO V. ILLINOIS*, 1964).

REMEMBER, AT FIRST ALL THESE PROTECTIONS APPLIED ONLY FOR TRIALS FOR FEDERAL CRIMES. STATE COURTS, MANY OF WHICH HAD THE POWER OF THE DEATH SENTENCE, WERE NOT BOUND TO OBSERVE THEM.

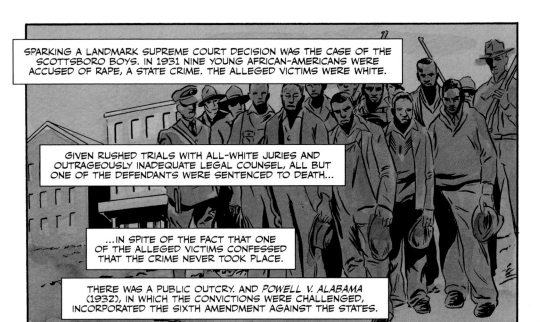

SPARKING A LANDMARK SUPREME COURT DECISION WAS THE CASE OF THE SCOTTSBORO BOYS. IN 1931 NINE YOUNG AFRICAN-AMERICANS WERE ACCUSED OF RAPE, A STATE CRIME. THE ALLEGED VICTIMS WERE WHITE.

GIVEN RUSHED TRIALS WITH ALL-WHITE JURIES AND OUTRAGEOUSLY INADEQUATE LEGAL COUNSEL, ALL BUT ONE OF THE DEFENDANTS WERE SENTENCED TO DEATH...

...IN SPITE OF THE FACT THAT ONE OF THE ALLEGED VICTIMS CONFESSED THAT THE CRIME NEVER TOOK PLACE.

THERE WAS A PUBLIC OUTCRY. AND *POWELL V. ALABAMA* (1932), IN WHICH THE CONVICTIONS WERE CHALLENGED, INCORPORATED THE SIXTH AMENDMENT AGAINST THE STATES.

BUT STATES WERE MADE TO PROVIDE COUNSEL ONLY IN CAPITAL CASES UNTIL *GIDEON V. WAINWRIGHT* (1963).

ALREADY BEHIND BARS, A FLORIDA MAN, TOO POOR TO HIRE A LAWYER, NEVERTHELESS MOUNTED A SUPREME COURT CHALLENGE OF HIS CONVICTION.

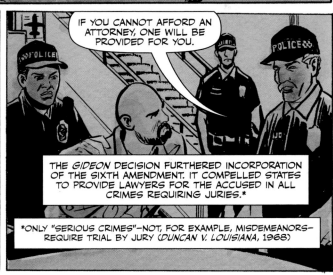

IF YOU CANNOT AFFORD AN ATTORNEY, ONE WILL BE PROVIDED FOR YOU.

THE *GIDEON* DECISION FURTHERED INCORPORATION OF THE SIXTH AMENDMENT. IT COMPELLED STATES TO PROVIDE LAWYERS FOR THE ACCUSED IN ALL CRIMES REQUIRING JURIES.*

*ONLY "SERIOUS CRIMES"—NOT, FOR EXAMPLE, MISDEMEANORS—REQUIRE TRIAL BY JURY (*DUNCAN V. LOUISIANA*, 1968)

American Justice

COMBO

HRU

2 3

ALL THESE PROTECTIONS BELONG TO THE ACCUSED, NOT THE PEOPLE. FOR INSTANCE, THE ACCUSED IS FREE TO WAIVE THE RIGHT TO A JURY TRIAL AND RECEIVE A BENCH TRIAL, WHERE A JUDGE HEARS THE CASE AND DECIDES THE VERDICT. THE ACCUSED MAY DECIDE A FAIR TRIAL IS IMPOSSIBLE IN THE DISTRICT WHERE THE ALLEGED CRIME TOOK PLACE, WAIVE THE RIGHT, AND APPLY FOR A CHANGE OF VENUE TO ANOTHER PLACE. THE RIGHT TO TRIAL MAY BE WAIVED ALTOGETHER WITH A PLEA BARGAIN. PLEADING GUILTY TO A CRIME IS, IN EFFECT, WAIVING THE RIGHT TO A TRIAL AND ACCEPTING THE SENTENCE.

The Seventh Amendment

ISSUES OF FAIR TRIALS PRESENTED ANOTHER MAJOR ANTI-FEDERALIST GRIEVANCE WITH THE CONSTITUTION.

IN ARTICLE III, WE HAVE THE PROVISION FOR TRIAL BY JURY IN CRIMINAL CASES...

...BUT WHERE IS THE SAME RIGHT FOR CIVIL CASES?

REMEMBER, IN A CIVIL CASE NEITHER OF THE PARTIES IN DISPUTE FACES GOING TO PRISON OR LOSING HIS LIFE.

WHAT'S AT ISSUE IS OFTEN MONEY—FOR EXAMPLE, ONE PARTY SEEKING *DAMAGES* TO BE PAID BY THE OTHER PARTY, FOR ALLEGED LOSS OF PROPERTY OR INJURY TO HEALTH.

SUCH A CASE SEEKING *MONETARY RELIEF* IS WHAT THE SEVENTH AMENDMENT REFERS TO AS A "SUIT AT COMMON LAW."

THIS IS DIFFERENT FROM AN EQUITY LAWSUIT, WHERE ONE PARTY IS, SAY, SEEKING A JUDGE TO COMMAND THE OTHER PARTY TO DO OR STOP DOING SOMETHING.

YOU ARE HEREBY ORDERED TO STOP CUTTING DOWN TREES ON THAT LAND.

CASES UNDER *EQUITY JURISDICTION* INCLUDE *CORPORATE LAW* AND *FAMILY LAW* MATTERS LIKE ADOPTION, DIVORCE, AND PROBATE.

EQUITY LAW CASES DO NOT REQUIRE A JURY.

DO NOT ENTER

PROPERTY MUST BE SECURED, OR LIBERTY CANNOT EXIST.

AMERICANS IN THE FOUNDING ERA PASSIONATELY BELIEVED IN THEIR RIGHT TO PROPERTY.

JOHN ADAMS, 1790.

AFTER ALL, MANY WHO COULD NOT HAVE DREAMED OF OWNING LAND IN BRITAIN DID FIND THAT OPPORTUNITY IN AMERICA.

PROPERTY RIGHTS ARE PROTECTED BY THE THIRD, FOURTH, AND FIFTH AMENDMENTS. THEY ARE ALSO ENSHRINED IN MANY STATE CONSTITUTIONS...

...Virginia: ...all men... have certain inherent rights... namely, the enjoyment of life and liberty, with the means of acquiring and possessing property...

...Pennsylvania: All men... have certain inherent and indefeasible rights, among which are... acquiring, possessing and protecting property...

THEY DEMANDED JURY TRIALS IN CASES THAT CAN DEPRIVE ONE OF LIFE AND LIBERTY (CRIMINAL SENTENCES OF DEATH OR IMPRISONMENT) AS WELL AS PROPERTY (FOR INSTANCE, DAMAGE AWARDS IN CIVIL CASES).

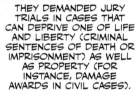

THE SEVENTH AMENDMENT GUARANTEES THIS.*

*IF THE AMOUNT OF MONEY IN DISPUTE EXCEEDS $20.

JURIES, IT WAS THOUGHT, WOULD BE CHECKS ON FEDERAL JUDGES, WHO OTHERWISE MIGHT BE SUBJECT TO BRIBES OR GOVERNMENT PRESSURE TO DECIDE CASES A CERTAIN WAY.

OBSERVING AMERICAN LIFE IN THE EARLY 19TH CENTURY, ALEXIS DE TOCQUEVILLE SUMMED UP ANOTHER TRUTH ABOUT JURIES.

Each man, in judging his neighbor, thinks that he may also be judged in his turn. It makes all feel that they have duties to fulfill towards society, and that they take part in government.

THE SECOND CLAUSE OF THE AMENDMENT ALSO DEALS WITH WHERE THE POWER OF THE JURY AND THE POWER OF A JUDGE ARE DRAWN.

IT REINS IN WAYS JUDGES MAY ORDER NEW TRIALS...

WE FIND THE DEFENDANT NOT GUILTY.

UNBELIEVABLE!

...AND, FOR EXAMPLE, DEALS WITH VERDICTS OR DAMAGE AWARDS THAT DO NOT SEEM JUSTIFIED BY THE EVIDENCE.

THE EIGHTH AMENDMENT

IT FOLLOWS FROM THE PRESUMPTION OF INNOCENCE THAT ACCUSED CRIMINALS SHOULD NOT HAVE TO SIT IN JAIL, ENDLESSLY AWAITING TRIAL.

AFTER ALL, PUTTING SOMEONE IN JAIL HARMS HIS OR HER REPUTATION. IT MAY KEEP HIM OR HER FROM FINDING A GOOD LAWYER OR SUPPORTING A FAMILY.

BUT THE COURT NEEDS TO INSURE THAT ACCUSED CRIMINALS DO NOT RUN AWAY, THAT THEY APPEAR FOR ALL THE PROCEEDINGS NECESSARY FOR TRIAL.

BAIL IS A SYSTEM THAT COMPROMISES THESE NEEDS WITH THOSE OF THE INDIVIDUAL.

COMMONLY, BAIL IS AN AMOUNT OF MONEY DEPOSITED AT THE COURT. IF THE ACCUSED MEETS ALL OBLIGATIONS, THAT MONEY IS REFUNDED AT THE END OF THE TRIAL.

THE EIGHTH AMENDMENT GUARANTEES THAT BAIL NOT BE EXCESSIVE.

IT MUST BE REASONABLY PROPORTIONATE TO THE SERIOUSNESS OF THE CRIME AND TO INSURE THAT THE ACCUSED WILL RETURN FOR TRIAL.

THERE IS ALSO A PROHIBITION AGAINST EXCESSIVE FINES, IMPOSED, FOR EXAMPLE, TO PUNISH SOMEONE WHO DOES *NOT* APPEAR IN COURT.

SURRATT. BOOTH. HAROLD.

War Department, Washington, April 20, 1865.

$100,000 REWARD!

THE MURDERER

Of our late beloved President, Abraham Lincoln,

IS STILL AT LARGE.

$50,000 REWARD

Will be paid by this Department for his apprehension, in addition to any reward offered by Municipal Authorities or State Executives.

$25,000 REWARD

$25,000 REWARD

Will be paid for the apprehension of David C. Harold, another of Booth's accomplices.

BAIL ITSELF IS NOT A RIGHT.

A JUDGE CAN DENY BAIL FOR CAPITAL CRIMES, VIOLENT CRIMES, IF AN ACCUSED POSES A SERIOUS RISK OF FLIGHT, OR OTHER REASONS SET BY LAW.

THE EIGHTH AMENDMENT ALSO ACKNOWLEDGES A RIGHT TO BE PROTECTED FROM "CRUEL AND UNUSUAL PUNISHMENT" BY THE GOVERNMENT.

"UNUSUAL" REFERS TO A PUNISHMENT WITHOUT SOME KIND OF PRECEDENT, ONE THAT HAS NEVER BEEN IMPOSED BY A COURT BEFORE.

FROM THE "DEATH OF A THOUSAND CUTS" TO BEING BURNED AT THE STAKE, HISTORY IS CROWDED WITH EXAMPLES OF WHAT THE SUPREME COURT RULED AGAINST IN *WHITLEY V. ALBERS* (1986)...

..."THE UNNECESSARY AND WANTON INFLICTION OF PAIN."

PUNISHMENT MAY NOT BE "GREATLY DISPROPORTIONED TO THE OFFENSES CHARGED" (*WEEMS V. U.S.*, 1910)...

...AND IT DOES NOT HAVE TO INVOLVE PHYSICAL PAIN TO QUALIFY AS CRUEL.

IN *ROBINSON V. CALIFORNIA* (1962), THE SUPREME COURT DECLARED THAT THE 90-DAY PRISON SENTENCE GIVEN TO A MAN CONVICTED OF BEING "ADDICTED TO THE USE OF NARCOTICS" VIOLATED THE EIGHTH AMENDMENT.

THE *ROBINSON* DECISION ALSO INCORPORATED THE CRUEL AND UNUSUAL PUNISHMENT CLAUSE AGAINST THE STATES. *COOPER INDUSTRIES V. LEATHERMAN TOOL GROUP, INC.* (2001) DID THE SAME FOR THE EXCESSIVE FINES PROVISION.

113

IS *CAPITAL PUNISHMENT* CRUEL AND UNUSUAL?

IT IS PLAINLY PRESCRIBED IN THE CONSTITUTION'S FIFTH AMENDMENT.

MANY ACTIVISTS WOULD LIKE TO END CAPITAL PUNISHMENT. BUT IN MODERN SUPREME COURT CASES, BEGINNING WITH *GREGG V. GEORGIA* (1976), IT HAS BEEN RULED THAT IT DOES NOT VIOLATE THE EIGHTH AMENDMENT IF, AMONG OTHER CRITERIA, THE JURY HAS BEEN IMPARTIAL, HAS BEEN ALLOWED TO HEAR *MITIGATING CIRCUMSTANCES,* AND HAS NOT BEEN FORCED TO HAND DOWN THE SENTENCE, AS WELL AS IF THE SENTENCE IS NOT THE RESULT OF PREJUDICE OR EXCESSIVE FOR THE CRIME.

The Ninth Amendment

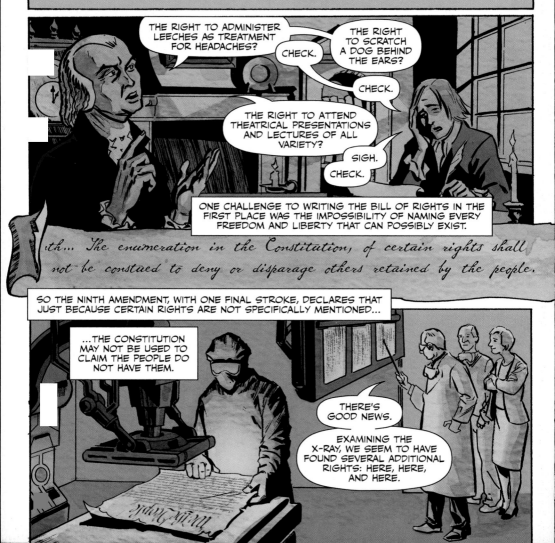

THE RIGHT TO ADMINISTER LEECHES AS TREATMENT FOR HEADACHES?

CHECK.

THE RIGHT TO SCRATCH A DOG BEHIND THE EARS?

CHECK.

THE RIGHT TO ATTEND THEATRICAL PRESENTATIONS AND LECTURES OF ALL VARIETY?

SIGH.

CHECK.

ONE CHALLENGE TO WRITING THE BILL OF RIGHTS IN THE FIRST PLACE WAS THE IMPOSSIBILITY OF NAMING EVERY FREEDOM AND LIBERTY THAT CAN POSSIBLY EXIST.

th... The enumeration in the Constitution, of certain rights shall not be construed to deny or disparage others retained by the people.

SO THE NINTH AMENDMENT, WITH ONE FINAL STROKE, DECLARES THAT JUST BECAUSE CERTAIN RIGHTS ARE NOT SPECIFICALLY MENTIONED...

...THE CONSTITUTION MAY NOT BE USED TO CLAIM THE PEOPLE DO NOT HAVE THEM.

THERE'S GOOD NEWS.

EXAMINING THE X-RAY, WE SEEM TO HAVE FOUND SEVERAL ADDITIONAL RIGHTS: HERE, HERE, AND HERE.

THOUGH IT TENDS TO COME UP RARELY, THE SUPREME COURT HAS RULED ON SPECIFIC, SO-CALLED *UNENUMERATED RIGHTS* SEVERAL TIMES...

...THE RIGHT TO ENGAGE IN POLITICAL ACTIVITY *(UNITED PUBLIC WORKERS V. MITCHELL, 1947)*...

...THE RIGHT OF THE PRESS TO REPORT CRIMINAL TRIALS *(RICHMOND NEWSPAPERS V. VIRGINIA, 1980)*...

...THE RIGHT FOR VOTES TO COUNT EQUALLY IN STATE ELECTORAL DISTRICTS *(REYNOLDS V. SIMS, 1964)*.

AND NOW NOBSCOT MOUNTAIN BEVERAGES PRESENTS...

...THE CONTINUING ADVENTURES OF THE MAN OF MYSTERY WHO STRIKES TERROR IN THE HEARTS OF AUTOCRATS, TYRANTS, AND DESPOTS EVERYWHERE...

...THE PENUMBRA!

HA HA HA HA HA.

WHO KNOWS WHAT OTHER RIGHTS LURK IN THE HEART OF THE CONSTITUTION?

WFSG

THE CONSTITUTION NEVER EXPLICITLY ACKNOWLEDGES A RIGHT TO PRIVACY...

...BUT WHEN YOU LOOK AT CERTAIN RIGHTS IN COMBINATION WITH ONE ANOTHER, IT SEEMS THAT OTHER RIGHTS ARE NATURALLY BUILT INTO THE DOCUMENT.

THE PENUMBRA KNOWS!

15¢

THE WORD *"PENUMBRA"*—FROM THE TERM FOR THE SHADED, OUTER AREA OF A SHADOW—HAS OFTEN BEEN USED TO DESCRIBE THIS IDEA OF BUILT-IN, UNSPECIFIED RIGHTS.

THE FIRST, THIRD, AND FOURTH AMENDMENTS ALL PROTECT PRIVACY. SO WHEN THOSE ARE LOOKED AT WITH THE ADDITION OF THE NINTH AMENDMENT, TO MANY CONSTITUTIONAL THINKERS, A RIGHT TO PRIVACY APPEARS UNQUESTIONABLE.

THE CONCEPT OF THE PRIVACY RIGHT "PENUMBRA" HAS INFORMED MANY LANDMARK SUPREME COURT DECISIONS.

FOR EXAMPLE, CONNECTICUT STATE LAW HELD THAT USING CONTRACEPTIVES—EVEN FOR MARRIED PEOPLE—OR TEACHING OTHER PEOPLE HOW TO USE THEM WAS ILLEGAL.

A BIRTH CONTROL ADVOCATE AND A MEDICAL DOCTOR, CONVICTED FOR VIOLATING THIS LAW, WON THEIR SUPREME COURT APPEAL. THE LAW WAS STRUCK DOWN IN *GRISWOLD V. CONNECTICUT* (1965).

THE NINTH AMENDMENT AND THE RIGHT TO PRIVACY ALSO PLAYED IN THE STILL-CONTROVERSIAL 7-2 *ROE V. WADE* (1974) DECISION, WHICH MADE MOST ANTIABORTION STATUTES ILLEGAL.

THE HIGH COURT WENT ON TO RECOGNIZE RIGHTS OF GAY PEOPLE IN THE 6-3 DECISION OF *LAWRENCE V. TEXAS* (2003).

THE LIBERTY PROTECTED BY THE CONSTITUTION ALLOWS HOMOSEXUAL PERSONS THE RIGHT TO CHOOSE TO ENTER UPON RELATIONSHIPS IN THE CONFINES OF THEIR HOMES AND THEIR OWN PRIVATE LIVES AND STILL RETAIN THEIR DIGNITY AS FREE PERSONS.

SUPREME COURT DECISIONS ARE NOT ALWAYS POPULAR...

...AND THERE ARE MANY WHO, ON THE BASIS OF ALTERNATE CONSTITUTIONAL INTERPRETATIONS, AS WELL AS ETHICAL AND RELIGIOUS VALUES, VOCALLY TAKE ISSUE WITH THEM.

BUT IN THE WORDS OF A 1992 CASE...

...THIS COURT'S OBLIGATION IS TO DEFINE THE LIBERTY OF ALL; NOT TO MANDATE ITS OWN MORAL CODE!

IN A WAY, THE TENTH AMENDMENT DOES FOR THE STATES WHAT THE REST OF THE BILL OF RIGHTS DOES FOR THE PEOPLE.

IT REITERATES THAT THE STATES, OR THE PEOPLE, HAVE ALL THE POWER EXCEPT FOR WHAT THE CONSTITUTION GIVES THE FEDERAL GOVERNMENT.*

THERE YOU GO...HELP YOURSELF.

*AND WHAT IT SAYS THE STATES CAN'T DO.

PSSST... ...DON'T WRITE THE WORD "EXPRESSLY"!

REMEMBER, THE BILL OF RIGHTS HAD ITS ORIGINS IN THE CONCERNS OF ANTI-FEDERALISTS. THE TENTH AMENDMENT WAS ANOTHER MEASURE TO SET TO REST THEIR FEARS ABOUT THE NEW GOVERNMENT, PARTICULARLY THAT THERE WAS NOT A BIG CONSPIRACY GOING ON TO ROB THE STATES OF ALL THEIR POWER.

STILL, THERE IS AN ARGUMENT TO BE MADE THAT THE TENTH AMENDMENT WAS LEFT VAGUE ON PURPOSE. THE FEDERALISTS WANTED BROAD POWERS FOR THE GOVERNMENT...EVEN ONES THE CONSTITUTION ONLY IMPLIES. AND THEY REMEMBERED ANOTHER FLAW IN THE ARTICLES OF CONFEDERATION.

ARTICLES OF CONFEDERATION

expressly delegated

WITH THESE WORDS, THE ARTICLES TOOK AWAY ROOM FOR INTERPRETATION OF THE NATIONAL GOVERNMENT'S POWER.

BY LEAVING OUT THE WORD "EXPRESSLY" IN THE TENTH AMENDMENT, THE FEDERALISTS LEFT THEMSELVES SOME LATITUDE.

COMMERCE CLAUSE

BASKET CLAUSE

SINCE THE RATIFICATION OF THE BILL OF RIGHTS...

...THERE HAS BEEN A LONG HISTORY OF POWER STRUGGLE BETWEEN THE FEDERAL AND STATE GOVERNMENTS...

...AND THERE IS NO DOUBT THAT THE FEDERAL GOVERNMENT IS MUCH MORE POWERFUL TODAY THAN WHEN IT BEGAN.

REMEMBER, THE NATION WAS IN PART FOUNDED ON THE IDEA OF SEPARATION OF POWERS...

...NOT JUST THE "HORIZONTAL" SEPARATION AMONG THE THREE BRANCHES OF FEDERAL GOVERNMENT, BUT THE "VERTICAL" SEPARATION BETWEEN IT AND THE STATES. THEIR ALL BEING CHECKED MAKES THE PEOPLE MORE FREE.

PLUS, A GOOD ARGUMENT FOR CHAMPIONS OF STATES' RIGHTS IS THAT THE LESS SUPERVISED THE STATES ARE, THE MORE THEY CAN BECOME "LABORATORIES OF DEMOCRACY"...

...EXPERIMENTING WITH LAWS AND IDEAS THAT, IF SUCCESSFUL, OTHERS CAN FOLLOW.

BUT CONSIDER AN ARGUMENT AGAINST STATES' RIGHTS. WITHOUT A FEDERAL GOVERNMENT TO MAKE LAWS LIKE THE CLEAN AIR ACT AND THE ENDANGERED SPECIES ACT AND TO APPLY A NATIONAL MINIMUM WAGE IN ALL FIFTY STATES...

...STATES COULD WIND UP COMPETING IN A *RACE TO THE BOTTOM* AS THEY TRY TO LURE BUSINESS AND TAX DOLLARS TO THEIR OWN BORDERS.

DON'T LIKE THE ENVIRONMENTAL LAWS OVER THERE?

C'MON OVER TO OUR STATE. WE'LL LET YOU CUT DOWN ALL THE FORESTS YOU WANT!

DON'T LIKE THE LABOR REGULATIONS OVER THERE?

C'MON OVER TO OUR STATE. WE'LL LET YOU TREAT YOUR WORKERS HOWEVER YOU WANT!

OUT OF BUSINESS

IT WAS STATES' RIGHTS ADVOCATES WHO WERE INSTRUMENTAL IN RATIFYING AN AMENDMENT TO REPEAL A PART OF THE CONSTITUTION'S ARTICLE III.

between a state and citizens of another state

IN *CHISHOLM V. GEORGIA* (1793), THE SUPREME COURT AFFIRMED THAT CITIZENS COULD SUE STATES IN FEDERAL COURT.

THE 11TH AMENDMENT (1795) EFFECTIVELY GAVE STATES IMMUNITY TO THIS PRACTICE...

...OBLIGATING CITIZENS TO SUE STATES ONLY IN STATE COURTS.

REMEMBER, THE TUMULTUOUS ELECTION OF 1800 PRODUCED AN ELECTORAL TIE BETWEEN THE CANDIDATES THOMAS JEFFERSON AND AARON BURR, THROWING THE DECISION TO CONGRESS...

...AND CONTRIBUTING YEARS LATER TO THE DUEL BETWEEN ALEXANDER HAMILTON AND BURR THAT TOOK HAMILTON'S LIFE.

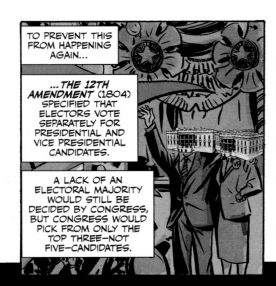

TO PREVENT THIS FROM HAPPENING AGAIN...

...*THE 12TH AMENDMENT* (1804) SPECIFIED THAT ELECTORS VOTE SEPARATELY FOR PRESIDENTIAL AND VICE PRESIDENTIAL CANDIDATES.

A LACK OF AN ELECTORAL MAJORITY WOULD STILL BE DECIDED BY CONGRESS, BUT CONGRESS WOULD PICK FROM ONLY THE TOP THREE—NOT FIVE—CANDIDATES.

BESIDES IMPOSING THE SAME QUALIFICATIONS TO HOLD OFFICE ON THE VICE PRESIDENT AS THE PRESIDENT...

...THE AMENDMENT ALSO STRONGLY ENCOURAGES THEM TO BE FROM DIFFERENT STATES.

THE RECONSTRUCTION AMENDMENTS: 13–15

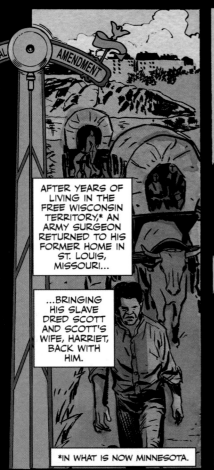

AFTER YEARS OF LIVING IN THE FREE WISCONSIN TERRITORY,* AN ARMY SURGEON RETURNED TO HIS FORMER HOME IN ST. LOUIS, MISSOURI...

...BRINGING HIS SLAVE DRED SCOTT AND SCOTT'S WIFE, HARRIET, BACK WITH HIM.

*IN WHAT IS NOW MINNESOTA.

SOON IN THE HANDS OF A NEW MASTER, SCOTT SUED FOR HIS FREEDOM, ARGUING THAT HAVING BEEN TAKEN FROM SLAVE TO FREE SOIL, HE AND HIS FAMILY WERE NO LONGER ANYONE'S PROPERTY.

SCOTT'S CASE REACHED THE SUPREME COURT IN 1856.

CHIEF JUSTICE ROGER B. TANEY RULED THAT SCOTT COULD NOT SUE IN THE SUPREME COURT AT ALL BECAUSE BLACK PEOPLE— EVEN FREE ONES—WERE NOT CITIZENS OF THE UNITED STATES...

...EVEN THOUGH BLACKS HAD FOUGHT IN THE REVOLUTION AND MANY STATE CONSTITUTIONS RECOGNIZED FREE BLACKS AS CITIZENS.

TANEY'S RULING ALSO DECLARED CONGRESS HAD NO POWER TO DECLARE SLAVERY ILLEGAL IN THE WEST, AS IT HAD IN THE 1820 *MISSOURI COMPROMISE.*

THE CASE CAME AT A TIME WHEN THE NORTH AND SOUTH WERE BITTERLY DIVIDED.

ON THE FLOOR OF THE U.S. SENATE, THE SOUTH CAROLINA SENATOR PRESTON BROOKS NEARLY BEAT TO DEATH THE MASSACHUSETTS ABOLITIONIST SENATOR CHARLES SUMNER.

DRED SCOTT V. SANDFORD DRAMATICALLY AFFECTED THE ELECTION OF ABRAHAM LINCOLN IN 1860 AND DEEPENED THE DISCORD. LINCOLN WAS ELECTED DESPITE NINE SOUTHERN STATES' NOT EVEN PUTTING HIM ON THE BALLOT.

LIVID, SOUTH CAROLINA BECAME THE FIRST STATE TO SECEDE FROM THE UNION, ON DECEMBER 20, 1860.

THE CIVIL WAR THAT FOLLOWED LASTED FOUR YEARS.

IT TOOK THE LIVES OF 620,000 AMERICANS.

AFRICAN-AMERICAN SOLDIERS, MANY JOINING AFTER LINCOLN'S *EMANCIPATION PROCLAMATION*, MADE UP APPROXIMATELY 10% OF THE U.S. ARMY.

LINCOLN REPORTED THAT MANY OF HIS FIELD COMMANDERS BELIEVED THAT "THE USE OF COLORED TROOPS CONSTITUTE THE HEAVIEST BLOWS YET DEALT TO THE REBELLION."

ALLOWING THAT IN GENERAL, WHITES WERE FIGHTING MORE TO PRESERVE THE UNION THAN END SLAVERY, LINCOLN NEVERTHELESS WROTE...

... "Why should they do anything for us if we will do nothing for them? if they stake their lives for us they must be prompted by the strongest motive, even the promise of freedom. And the promise, being made, must be kept."

COMING AFTER THE END OF THE FIGHTING, AND EVEN THE ASSASSINATION OF PRESIDENT LINCOLN...

...*THE 13TH AMENDMENT* (1865) ELIMINATED FOREVER SLAVERY, AND ANY OTHER KIND OF FORCED OR INVOLUNTARY LABOR, ON AMERICAN SOIL.

THE LABOR OF CONVICTED CRIMINALS IN PRISON IS, HOWEVER, CLEARLY EXCEPTED...

...AS IS MILITARY SERVICE FOR THOSE WHO ARE DRAFTED*...

U.S. V. HOLMES (1968).

...AND JURY SERVICE.*

BUTLER V. PERRY (1916).

JURY DUTY
LINE FORMS HERE

Subject to its jurisdiction thereof

...AT LEAST FOR THOSE UNDER U.S. JURISDICTION.

AT THE TIME THIS EXEMPTED NATIVE AMERICANS.

THE FIRST PART OF *THE 14TH AMENDMENT* (1868) IS A DIRECT COUNTERPUNCH TO *DRED SCOTT V. SANDFORD*. APPLYING RETROACTIVELY TO ALL THE NEWLY FREED SLAVES, IT STATES THAT U.S. CITIZENSHIP IS A BIRTHRIGHT...

RIGHTS OF CITIZENSHIP WERE TO BE WITHHELD FROM THEM UNTIL THE 1924 *INDIAN CITIZENSHIP ACT.*

THE AMENDMENT EXTENDS TO THE NATURALIZED, THOSE BORN ELSEWHERE WHO COMPLETE THE LEGAL PROCESS OF BECOMING CITIZENS.

WE HAVE ALREADY EXAMINED HOW THE 14TH AMENDMENT BLOCKS STATES FROM TAKING ACTIONS THAT DENY PEOPLE CIVIL RIGHTS.

NOW WE KNOW WHY: TO BRING FORMER SLAVES FULLY INTO THE FOLD OF U.S. CITIZENSHIP.

IT APPLIES AS WELL TO MALE AND FEMALE, RICH AND POOR, AND CITIZENS BORN AT HOME OR ABROAD.

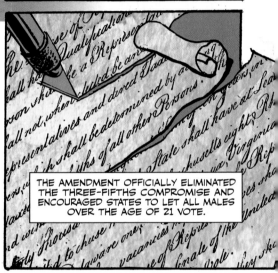

THE AMENDMENT OFFICIALLY ELIMINATED THE THREE-FIFTHS COMPROMISE AND ENCOURAGED STATES TO LET ALL MALES OVER THE AGE OF 21 VOTE.

AN OTHERWISE UNENFORCED CLAUSE OF SECTION 2 OF THE AMENDMENT ALLOWS STATES TO DENY CONVICTED FELONS THEIR VOTING RIGHTS EVEN AFTER THEY HAVE SERVED THEIR SENTENCES.*

RICHARDSON V. RAMIREZ (1974).

UNDER SECTION 3 OF THE AMENDMENT, ANYONE WHO HAD BEEN INVOLVED IN THE REBELLION OF THE SOUTH—AS A PARTICIPANT OR AS A PROVIDER OF "AID OR COMFORT"—COULD NOT HOLD FEDERAL OR STATE OFFICE.

THIRTY YEARS LATER, CONGRESS STRUCK THIS DOWN.

IN SECTION 4, THE UNITED STATES REFUSED TO TAKE RESPONSIBILITY FOR THE CONFEDERACY'S WAR DEBT.

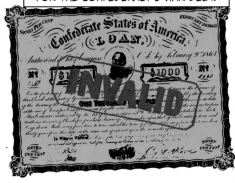

AS FOR REPARATIONS TO SLAVE MASTERS FOR THE LOSS OF THEIR "PROPERTY," THEY WERE NOT TO BE PAID. IN FACT, ANY SUCH CLAIM WOULD BE ILLEGAL AND VOID.

THE LAST OF THE RECONSTRUCTION-ERA AMENDMENTS WAS THE *15TH AMENDMENT* (1870).

APPLYING TO BOTH THE STATES AND THE FEDERAL GOVERNMENT, IT BESTOWED FULL VOTING RIGHTS ON ALL MEN, REGARDLESS OF RACE, COLOR, OR AN INDIVIDUAL'S EVER HAVING BEEN A SLAVE.

SINCE ENFORCING THE 13TH, 14TH, AND 15TH AMENDMENTS DID NOT INVOLVE POWERS ALREADY GIVEN TO CONGRESS BY THE CONSTITUTION...

ON THE SURFACE, THE RATIFICATION OF THESE AMENDMENTS WOULD SEEM AN INCREDIBLE LEAP FORWARD IN "LIBERTY AND JUSTICE" FOR FORMER SLAVES.

...CLAUSES HAD TO BE ADDED TO EACH OF THEM (AND LATER TO THE 19TH, 23RD, 24TH, AND 26TH AMENDMENTS) TO MAKE THAT POSSIBLE.

BUT THE REALITY IS THAT FOR MANY, THE DECADES RIGHT AFTER THE CIVIL WAR...

...WERE ANYTHING BUT.

AAAAIIYY!

THE WAR, AND THE POLICIES OF THE *RADICAL REPUBLICANS* IN THE U.S. CONGRESS AFTER IT, TURNED THE SOUTH'S ENTIRE WAY OF LIFE UPSIDE DOWN.

OFTEN BANKRUPT, CROPS ROTTING IN THE FIELDS, FRIENDS AND RELATIVES KILLED IN BATTLE, THEIR SENSE OF SELF SHATTERED...

...SOUTHERN WHITES TURNED TO INTIMIDATION AND VIOLENCE TO CRUSH THE NEWLY EMPOWERED BLACK CITIZENS.

POLL TAXES, LITERACY TESTS, AND OTHER COOKED-UP QUALIFICATIONS TO VOTE SOON KEPT MANY OF THEM FROM THE POLLS...

...AND A FEDERAL GOVERNMENT MORE CONCERNED WITH REBUILDING THE UNION THAN INTEGRATING AFRICAN-AMERICANS CONTRIBUTED LITTLE HELP.

PLANTATIONS SEIZED BY THE UNION ARMY AND GRANTED TO FREED SLAVES—THE SO-CALLED FORTY ACRES AND A MULE POLICY—WERE RETURNED, BY FORCE, TO THEIR FORMER OWNERS.

PRESIDENT ANDREW JOHNSON, A TENNESSEAN ONCE OPPOSED TO THE UPPER CLASS OF THE SOUTH, ISSUED PARDONS TO HUNDREDS OF FORMER CONFEDERATES EVERY DAY.

WITH NO LAND, SPOTTY EDUCATION IF AT ALL, AND NOWHERE TO GO, MANY FORMER SLAVES WENT BACK TO WORK FOR THEIR OLD MASTERS FOR WAGES NEARLY TOO LOW TO LIVE ON.

ON TOP OF ALL THIS, THE SUPREME COURT'S INTERPRETATION OF THE 14TH AMENDMENT WHITTLED DOWN THE IDEA OF EQUAL PROTECTION TO ALMOST NOTHING.

FROM MISSISSIPPI, JOHN ROY LYNCH, ELECTED TO THE U.S. HOUSE OF REPRESENTATIVES IN 1872...

FORTY-THIRD CONGRESS. SESS. II. CH. 114. 1875.

...HELPED PASS THE 1875 *CIVIL RIGHTS ACT*, MEANT TO GIVE ALL PEOPLE EQUAL ACCESS TO ALL PUBLIC PLACES...

... That all persons within the jurisdiction of the United States shall be entitled to the full and equal enjoyment of the accommodations, advantages, facilities, and privileges of inns, public conveyances on land or water, theaters, and other places of public amusement; subject only to the conditions and limitations established by law, and applicable alike to citizens of every race and color, regardless of any previous condition of servitude.

IT WOULD BE RUNNING THE SLAVERY ARGUMENT INTO THE GROUND TO MAKE IT APPLY TO EVERY ACT OF DISCRIMINATION WHICH A PERSON MAY SEE FIT TO MAKE...IN... MATTERS OF INTERCOURSE OR BUSINESS.

IN 1883 THE SUPREME COURT STRUCK THIS DOWN AS UNCONSTITUTIONAL.

THE 8-1 DECISION HELD THAT THE 14TH AMENDMENT APPLIED ONLY TO THE "OPERATIONS" AND "ACTIONS" OF STATE GOVERNMENT, NOT OF PRIVATE CITIZENS OR PRIVATE BUSINESSES.

EAST LOUISIANA RAILROAD
FIRST CLASS—NOT TRANSFERABLE. No 1970

LATER *PLESSY V. FERGUSON* (1896), UPHOLDING THE CONVICTION OF A BLACK MAN WHO DARED SIT IN A TRAIN'S "WHITES ONLY" SECTION...

...BEGAN THE RULE OF SEPARATE BUT EQUAL, *SEGREGATION* OF SCHOOLS, RESTAURANTS, PUBLIC BATHROOMS...

PROGRESSIVE ERA AMENDMENTS

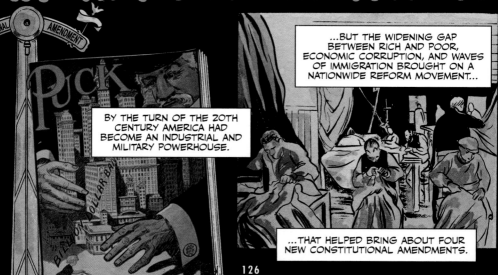

BY THE TURN OF THE 20TH CENTURY AMERICA HAD BECOME AN INDUSTRIAL AND MILITARY POWERHOUSE.

...BUT THE WIDENING GAP BETWEEN RICH AND POOR, ECONOMIC CORRUPTION, AND WAVES OF IMMIGRATION BROUGHT ON A NATIONWIDE REFORM MOVEMENT...

...THAT HELPED BRING ABOUT FOUR NEW CONSTITUTIONAL AMENDMENTS.

THE **16TH AMENDMENT** (1913) GAVE CONGRESS NEW POWERS TO TAX INCOMES OF INDIVIDUALS AND CORPORATIONS— WITHOUT HAVING TO PAY ATTENTION TO A STATE'S POPULATION.

POLLOCK V. FARMERS' LOAN & TRUST CO. (1895).

SPRINGER V. U.S. (1881).

DID CONGRESS HAVE THE RIGHT TO TAX INCOME DIRECTLY? HAVING ALL BUT CONTRADICTED ITSELF, THE SUPREME COURT ULTIMATELY HELD THAT THE GOVERNMENT'S MOST RECENT ATTEMPT TO DO SO WAS UNCONSTITUTIONAL.

MORE THAN A HUNDRED YEARS AFTER THE RATIFICATION OF THE CONSTITUTION, MOST AMERICANS BELIEVED THE GOVERNMENT IT SET UP HAD PROVED ITSELF.

THE POWER OF THE STATES WAS ON THE WANE.

...AND IN LIGHT OF BRIBERY SCANDALS THAT HAD TAINTED THE ELECTIONS OF SENATORS...

...THE 17TH AMENDMENT (1913) TOOK THE LEAD OF OREGON, NEBRASKA, AND OTHER STATES. FROM NOW ON THE PEOPLE—NOT THEIR STATE LEGISLATORS—WOULD ELECT U.S. SENATORS.

FOR GENERATIONS, MEMBERS OF THE *TEMPERANCE MOVEMENT* BLAMED THE CONSUMPTION OF ALCOHOL FOR CRIME, DISEASE, MENTAL ILLNESS, UNEMPLOYMENT, AND A HOST OF ILLS PLAGUING SOCIETY.

SOMETIMES BORDERING ON THE FANATICAL, THE VARIOUS GROUPS WERE IMMENSELY SUCCESSFUL IN GETTING THEIR MESSAGE OUT.

THROUGH THEIR EFFORTS, THE *18TH AMENDMENT* (1919) MADE ILLEGAL THE MAKING, TRANSPORTING, AND SELLING OF ALCOHOLIC BEVERAGES. THE ERA OF *PROHIBITION* BEGAN.

THE ENGLISH PAINTER G. E. HICKS COMPOSED A SERIES OF PAINTINGS IN 1863, TOGETHER TITLED *WOMAN'S MISSION*.

THEY REVEAL SOCIETY'S IDEAS ABOUT THE ROLE OF WOMEN AT THE TIME...

...THAT THEIR PLACE WAS ONLY AS MOTHERS, WIVES, AND DAUGHTERS.

WOMEN HAVE SOMETIMES BEEN CALLED THE 51% MINORITY. THEY SLIGHTLY OUTNUMBER MEN, BUT IN THE EYES OF THE LAW HAD FOR HUNDREDS OF YEARS BEEN CONSIDERED THE PROPERTY OF THEIR HUSBANDS OR FATHERS.

ELIZABETH CADY STANTON, A WOMAN WHO HAD GROWN UP REPEATEDLY HEARING THE WORDS "I WISH YOU WERE A BOY" FROM HER FATHER...

...CALLED A CONVENTION IN SENECA FALLS, NEW YORK, IN 1848. AT ITS END THE CONVENTION ISSUED A DECLARATION CALLING FOR WOMEN'S EQUALITY—EVEN THE RIGHT TO VOTE.

FIRST CONVENTION FOR **WOMAN'S RIGHTS** WAS HELD ON THIS CORNER 1848

IN 1851 STANTON BECAME THE MENTOR OF SUSAN B. ANTHONY. A QUAKER AND FORMER TEACHER, ANTHONY CAME FROM A RELIGIOUS COMMUNITY WHERE WOMEN AND MEN WERE SEEN TO BE EQUAL IN THE EYES OF GOD.

TOGETHER THE TWO CAMPAIGNED FOR TEMPERANCE, ABOLITION OF SLAVERY, AND WOMEN'S RIGHTS, ANTHONY BECOMING FAMOUS FOR HER TIRELESSNESS. THEY FORMED THE NATIONAL WOMAN SUFFRAGE ASSOCIATION (LATER TO BECOME NAWSA) AS A RESULT OF FEELING BETRAYED THAT THE 15TH AMENDMENT, WHICH THEY HAD FOUGHT SO HARD FOR, DID NOT EXTEND THE VOTE TO WOMEN. STANTON AUTHORED A PROPOSED CONSTITUTIONAL AMENDMENT THAT, FOR THE NEXT 40 YEARS, WAS SUBMITTED TO EVERY SESSION OF CONGRESS.

NEITHER ELIZABETH CADY STANTON NOR SUSAN ANTHONY LIVED TO SEE THE DAY ALL WOMEN COULD VOTE.

WE DEMAND AN AMENDMENT TO THE CONSTITUTION OF THE UNITED STATES ENFRANCHISING THE WOMEN OF THIS COUNTRY

ALTHOUGH SOME STATES HAD PERMITTED WOMEN TO VOTE AND HOLD OFFICE, THE WYOMING TERRITORY BEING THE FIRST, IN 1869...

BALLOT BOX

...*THE 19TH AMENDMENT* (1920) MADE IT UNIFORM FEDERAL LAW.

MORE THAN A HUNDRED YEARS' WORTH OF TRANS-PORTATION AND COMMUNICATION ADVANCES PAVED THE WAY FOR THE *20TH AMENDMENT* (1933).

HONK! HONK!

HONK!

WITH THERE NO LONGER BEING A NEED FOR THE PRESIDENT AND VICE PRESIDENT TO WAIT FOR SPRING BEFORE THEY COULD LEAVE WASHINGTON, D.C., AND GO HOME, THE DAY THE PRESIDENT AND VICE PRESIDENT TAKE OFFICE WAS MOVED FROM MARCH 4 TO JANUARY 20. CONGRESS WOULD NOW BEGIN ON JANUARY 3.

REDUCING THE AMOUNT OF TIME POLITICIANS WHO HAVE LOST THEIR MOST RECENT ELECTIONS MUST SPEND IN OFFICE, THIS IS SOMETIMES CALLED THE LAME DUCK AMENDMENT.

QUACK!

QUACK!

QUACK!

IT ALSO COVERS SOME *PRESIDENTIAL SUCCESSION* SCENARIOS THAT TO DATE HAVE NOT COME INTO PLAY.

FOR EXAMPLE, IF I DIE BEFORE I CAN BE INAUGURATED, THIS GUY HERE BECOMES PRESIDENT...

...AND CONGRESS CAN COME UP WITH A PLAN IF EVEN I AM NOT ABLE TO TAKE OFFICE.

FOURTEEN YEARS EARLIER THOSE WHO HAD PUSHED FOR PROHIBITION WERE CELEBRATING.

THE REIGN OF TEARS IS OVER! THE SLUMS WILL SOON BE ONLY A MEMORY. WE WILL TURN OUR PRISONS INTO FACTORIES AND OUR JAILS INTO STOREHOUSES AND CORNCRIBS!

BUT CONSUMPTION OF ALCOHOL HARDLY ENDED.

KNOCK

KNOCK KNOCK

KNOCK

IT JUST WENT UNDERGROUND.

AND THAT DIDN'T MAKE THINGS BETTER.

130

IT MADE THEM WORSE.

GANGWAY!

SKREEEE!

ACK ACK ACK ACK ACK ACK ACK ACK ACK ACK ACK ACK ACK ACK ACK!

IT WAS ALSO A MONEYMAKING BONANZA FOR *ORGANIZED CRIME*, WHICH SOLD ALCOHOL ON THE BLACK MARKET.

WITH SO MUCH MONEY ON THE TABLE, CORRUPTION SPREAD WITH MANY JUDGES, POLITICIANS, AND POLICE OFFICERS WILLING TO TAKE A BRIBE TO LOOK THE OTHER WAY.

THERE IS NOT LESS DRUNKENNESS IN THE REPUBLIC, BUT MORE. THERE IS NOT LESS CRIME, BUT MORE. THERE IS NOT LESS INSANITY, BUT MORE. THE COST OF GOVERNMENT IS NOT SMALLER, BUT VASTLY GREATER. RESPECT FOR LAW HAS NOT INCREASED, BUT DIMINISHED.

JOURNALIST H. L. MENCKEN, 1925.

WITH THE NATION ALSO IN THE GRIPS OF THE *GREAT DEPRESSION* AND HOPING TO MAKE LEGAL MONEY FROM THE PRODUCTION AND SALE OF ALCOHOL AGAIN...

IN COMPLIANCE WITH THE 18 AMENDMENT NO INTOXICATING LIQUOR ALLOWED ON THE PREMISES

...*THE 21ST AMENDMENT* (1933) WAS NEEDED TO REPEAL THE 18TH.

THE 21ST IS THE ONLY AMENDMENT THAT WENT INTO EFFECT UNDER ARTICLE V'S PROVISION FOR RATIFICATION BY STATE CONVENTIONS.

ONE CONSISTENT ANTI-FEDERALIST RANT HAD ALWAYS BEEN THAT THE CONSTITUTION DID NOT SET A TERM LIMIT FOR THE PRESIDENCY.

BY HIS EXAMPLE, HOWEVER, GEORGE WASHINGTON SET AN UNOFFICIAL PRECEDENT FOR SERVING NO MORE THAN TWO TERMS.

PRESIDENT FRANKLIN D. ROOSEVELT, WHO LED THE COUNTRY BOTH THROUGH THE GREAT DEPRESSION...

...AND MOST OF *WORLD WAR II*, WON NOT ONLY AN UNPRECEDENTED THIRD TERM IN 1940 BUT A FOURTH TERM IN 1944. AT 63 AND IN POOR HEALTH, HE DIED FOUR MONTHS INTO THAT FOURTH TERM.

ROOSEVELT AND HIS SUCCESSOR, HARRY TRUMAN, WERE BOTH DEMOCRATS...

...BUT THE 80TH U.S. CONGRESS-ELECTED IN 1946 WITH 58 MORE HOUSE MEMBERS AND 6 MORE SENATORS THAN THEIR OPPONENTS—WAS REPUBLICAN.

CONGRESS PROPOSED THE *22ND AMENDMENT* (1951), LIMITING ELECTED PRESIDENTS TO TWO TERMS IN OFFICE.

HOWEVER, IF THE PRESIDENCY BECOMES VACANT, AND A VICE PRESIDENT OR OTHER SUCCESSOR SERVES TWO YEARS OR LESS OF HIS PREDECESSOR'S TERM, THAT PERSON MAY RUN FOR TWO FULL TERMS, EQUALING A POSSIBLE TOTAL OF TEN YEARS IN OFFICE.

THE *23RD AMENDMENT* (1961) GAVE THE DISTRICT OF COLUMBIA AS MANY PRESIDENTIAL ELECTORS AS THE LEAST POPULOUS STATE, CURRENTLY THREE.

LACKING STATE STATUS, THE DISTRICT STILL HAS NO REPRESENTATION IN THE U.S. CONGRESS. THE GRANT OF ELECTORS WAS A RESPONSE TO RESIDENTS' ONGOING CONCERNS THAT THEY HAVE THE RESPONSIBILITIES OF U.S. CITIZENSHIP—FEDERAL TAXES AND ENROLLMENT IN ANY MILITARY DRAFT—WITHOUT ALL THE BENEFITS.

THE SEPARATE BUT EQUAL DOCTRINE, LEADING TO RACIAL SEGREGATION IN, AMONG OTHER PLACES, SCHOOLS, WAS NOT TO BE TORN DOWN UNTIL 1954.

A NUMBER OF LAWSUITS ARGUING THAT SEPARATE WAS IN FACT *NOT* EQUAL CAME BEFORE THE SUPREME COURT.

NOT ONLY HAD AMERICAN SCHOOLS BEEN SEGREGATED BY WHITE AND BLACK, BUT THE SOUTHWEST HAD UNDERFUNDED "MEXICAN SCHOOLS" FOR LATINOS.

A 1921 CALIFORNIA LAW SAID THE STATE COULD "ESTABLISH SEPARATE SCHOOLS FOR INDIAN CHILDREN AND FOR CHILDREN OF CHINESE, JAPANESE, OR MONGOLIAN PARENTAGE."

THE SUPREME COURT'S UNANIMOUS RULING IN *BROWN V. BOARD OF EDUCATION* (1954) WAS A POINTED REVERSAL OF *PLESSY V. FERGUSON.*

WE CONCLUDE THAT IN THE FIELD OF PUBLIC EDUCATION THE DOCTRINE OF "SEPARATE BUT EQUAL" HAS NO PLACE. SEPARATE EDUCATIONAL FACILITIES ARE INHERENTLY UNEQUAL.

RACE MIXING IS COMMUNISM

STOP THE RACE MIXING

RACE MIXING IS COMMUNISM

AGAIN, A SUPREME COURT DECISION DOES NOT ALWAYS LEAD TO INSTANT CHANGE IN SOCIETY.

PRESIDENT DWIGHT EISENHOWER HAD TO CALL IN THE ARMY TO HELP DESEGREGATE CENTRAL HIGH SCHOOL IN LITTLE ROCK, ARKANSAS, IN 1957.

THE STRUGGLE TO SECURE CIVIL RIGHTS FOR ALL BEGAN LONG BEFORE AND CONTINUES LONG AFTER *BROWN V. BOARD.*

REMEMBER, DURING RECONSTRUCTION, AS A WAY TO KEEP AFRICAN-AMERICANS FROM VOTING AND HOLDING OFFICE, MANY SOUTHERN STATES INSTITUTED A POLL TAX.

No. 838   Birmingham, Ala. 4/9 1896
Received of J. M. Arkins (Col.) (White.)
the sum of Two & 50 Dollars
in full of amount of Poll Tax for the year 1895.

Poll Tax,	1	50
Assessor's Fee,		50
Collector's Fee,		50

_____ P.T.C.

MANY POOR BLACKS COULD NOT AFFORD TO PAY THE FEES REQUIRED TO VOTE.

BY 1962 ONLY FIVE STATES STILL RETAINED A POLL TAX.

THE *24TH AMENDMENT* (1964), ANOTHER LEGACY OF THE CIVIL RIGHTS STRUGGLE, STAMPED OUT POLL TAXES OR ANY OTHER TAXES THAT COULD DENY OR ABRIDGE THE RIGHT TO VOTE.

EVEN MORE THAN THE 14TH AMENDMENT, IN MODERN TIMES IT HAS BEEN ARTICLE I'S COMMERCE CLAUSE THAT HAS LENT THE GOVERNMENT MUSCLE TO EXTEND CIVIL RIGHTS TO THE PRIVATE SPHERE.

BECAUSE OF CASES LIKE *HEART OF ATLANTA MOTEL V. U.S.* (1964) AND *KATZENBACH V. McCLUNG* (1964), BUSINESS OWNERS WHOSE PRODUCTS OR SERVICES AFFECT INTERSTATE BUSINESS—EVEN IN A MINOR WAY—MUST NOT CLOSE THEIR DOORS TO ANY CUSTOMERS ON THE BASIS OF RACE.

TWICE IN THE VICE PRESIDENTIAL CAREER OF RICHARD NIXON, HE RECEIVED A STARTLING PHONE CALL TELLING HIM TO PREPARE TO ASSUME THE PRESIDENCY.

PRESIDENT DWIGHT EISENHOWER SUFFERED A HEART ATTACK IN SEPTEMBER 1955 AND A STROKE IN 1957.

THE PRESIDENT SURVIVED BOTH HEALTH CRISES.

THE CONSTITUTION HAD INSTRUCTIONS FOR A PRESIDENT'S DEATH, RESIGNATION OR REMOVAL FROM OFFICE, BUT NOT FOR HIS INCAPACITATION...

...OR FOR ANY KIND OF VACANCY OF THE VICE PRESIDENCY.

EENIE, MEENIE, MINIE, MOE...

IN PART BASED ON PLANS MADE BY NIXON DURING EISENHOWER'S BRUSHES WITH DEATH, *THE 25TH AMENDMENT* (1967) CLARIFIED A PLAN OF SUCCESSION.

IF THERE IS A VACANCY IN THE VICE PRESIDENCY, THE PRESIDENT SELECTS A REPLACEMENT...

...SUBJECT TO A MAJORITY VOTE CONFIRMATION IN BOTH HOUSES OF CONGRESS.

NIXON HIMSELF CALLED ON THIS PROVISION WHEN, UPON THE RESIGNATION OF HIS OWN VICE PRESIDENT IN 1973, HE REPLACED HIM WITH GERALD R. FORD.

A LIVING PRESIDENT UNABLE TO PERFORM HIS DUTIES MUST TEMPORARILY STEP DOWN...

...AFTER THE PRESIDENT INFORMS THE PRESIDENT PRO TEM OF THE SENATE AND THE SPEAKER OF THE HOUSE OF HIS CONDITION.

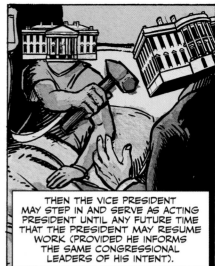

THEN THE VICE PRESIDENT MAY STEP IN AND SERVE AS ACTING PRESIDENT UNTIL ANY FUTURE TIME THAT THE PRESIDENT MAY RESUME WORK (PROVIDED HE INFORMS THE SAME CONGRESSIONAL LEADERS OF HIS INTENT).

THE AMENDMENT ALSO EMPOWERS THE VICE PRESIDENT TO ASSUME THE EXECUTIVE'S RESPONSIBILITIES...

...IF HE AND A MAJORITY OF THE CABINET MEMBERS AGREE THE PRESIDENT IS NOT FIT TO PERFORM THE OFFICE'S DUTIES.

CONGRESS CAN THEN BE CALLED ON, WITH A SUPERMAJORITY VOTE, TO BLOCK THE PRESIDENT'S INTENTIONS TO RETURN TO OFFICE.

NO... LISTEN TO ME...

...I'M FINE.

DROP THE BALLOT IN THE BOX WHEN YOU'RE DONE, DEARIE.

THANKS, MA'AM.

"OLD ENOUGH TO FIGHT, OLD ENOUGH TO VOTE" HAD BEEN A RALLYING CRY SINCE THE DAYS OF WORLD WAR II.

♪

BUT EVEN WELL INTO THE ERA OF THE VIETNAM CONFLICT...

GAH!

INCOMING!

SHHH SHHH

TAT TAT

TAT TAT TAT

HALT ALL A.R.A.! THIS IS A FRIENDLY POSITION! REPEAT! HALT ALL A.R.A.!

...YOUNG MEN UNDER THE AGE OF 21 COULD BE DRAFTED AND SENT TO WAR WITHOUT ANY SAY IN THE ELECTION OF OFFICIALS WHO HELD THEIR LIVES IN THEIR HANDS.

K-BOOM!

I SAID TO GET YOUR MACHINE GUN UP THAT HILL! NOW!

BUT... BUT...

YOU GOT ROCKS BETWEEN YOUR EARS, NEW GUY?

WHA...?

THE 26TH AMENDMENT (1971) RECONCILED THIS BY SETTING 18 AS THE MINIMUM VOTING AGE IN ALL ELECTIONS, FEDERAL, STATE, AND LOCAL.

THE 26TH AMENDMENT IS IN AN AMERICAN TRADITION, TAKING THOSE WHO CAME TO THE AID OF THE COUNTRY IN TIME OF WAR...

...AND HONORING THEM WITH THE VOTE.

THE MOST RECENT OF THE CONSTITUTIONAL AMENDMENTS HAD A LONG TIME TO WAIT BEFORE BEING GIVEN LIFE.

FIRST PROPOSED BY JAMES MADISON ALL THE WAY BACK IN 1789...

OH, NO, WE DON'T!

...THE 27TH AMENDMENT (1992) HELPS PREVENT CONGRESS FROM VOTING ITSELF A RAISE.

AS FOR ANY PAY HIKES IT PASSES...THEY MAY NOT TAKE EFFECT UNTIL THE NEXT SESSION.

BOTH IN ITS
INCEPTION...

...AND IN ITS
APPLICATION...

...THE CONSTITUTION
ENCOMPASSES THE
HIGHEST POINTS OF
AMERICAN HISTORY...

...AS WELL
AS THE
LOWEST.

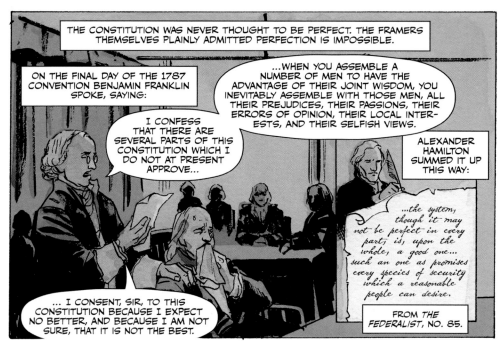

THE CONSTITUTION WAS NEVER THOUGHT TO BE PERFECT. THE FRAMERS THEMSELVES PLAINLY ADMITTED PERFECTION IS IMPOSSIBLE.

ON THE FINAL DAY OF THE 1787 CONVENTION BENJAMIN FRANKLIN SPOKE, SAYING:

I CONFESS THAT THERE ARE SEVERAL PARTS OF THIS CONSTITUTION WHICH I DO NOT AT PRESENT APPROVE...

...WHEN YOU ASSEMBLE A NUMBER OF MEN TO HAVE THE ADVANTAGE OF THEIR JOINT WISDOM, YOU INEVITABLY ASSEMBLE WITH THOSE MEN, ALL THEIR PREJUDICES, THEIR PASSIONS, THEIR ERRORS OF OPINION, THEIR LOCAL INTER-ESTS, AND THEIR SELFISH VIEWS.

ALEXANDER HAMILTON SUMMED IT UP THIS WAY:

...the system, though it may not be perfect in every part, is, upon the whole, a good one... such an one as promises every species of security which a reasonable people can desire.

FROM *THE FEDERALIST*, NO. 85.

... I CONSENT, SIR, TO THIS CONSTITUTION BECAUSE I EXPECT NO BETTER, AND BECAUSE I AM NOT SURE, THAT IT IS NOT THE BEST.

AT HEART, OUR FOUNDING DOCUMENT CREATES A SYSTEM, A PROCESS OF GOVERNMENT...

DO IT YOURSELF KIT THE UNITED STATES OF AMERICA

ASSEMBLY INSTALLATION INSTRUCTIONS

...THAT EMBODIES A SET OF SHARED VALUES.

TOGETHER, THEY COMPRISE A METHOD OF BALANCING INTERESTS AND ACCOMMODATING CHANGES, WITHOUT OCCASIONING THE VIOLENT UPHEAVALS SEEN IN SO MUCH OF HISTORY.

FOR GENERATIONS COURAGEOUS INDIVIDUALS–POLITICIANS, JUDGES, LAWYERS, AND EVERYDAY PEOPLE–HAVE APPLIED THOSE VALUES AND WORKED WITHIN THAT PROCESS...

...TO CONTINUE TO GUIDE THE CONSTITUTION OF THE UNITED STATES OF AMERICA ALWAYS IN THE DIRECTION OF, IF NOT A PERFECT UNION, THEN A "MORE PERFECT" UNION.

SUCH A FORWARD MARCH IS POSSIBLE ONLY WHEN...

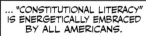

... "CONSTITUTIONAL LITERACY" IS ENERGETICALLY EMBRACED BY ALL AMERICANS.

IN THE WORDS OF ONE LONG-SERVING U.S. SENATOR...

"...WE CANNOT DEFEND AND PROTECT THIS DREAM IF WE ARE IGNORANT OF THE CONSTITUTION'S HISTORY AND HOW IT WORKS."

We the People

"IGNORANCE IS ULTIMATELY THE WORST ENEMY OF A PEOPLE WHO WANT TO BE FREE."

RECOMMENDED READING

ACKNOWLEDGMENTS

RECOMMENDED READING

The number of books written about the Constitution of the United States is staggering: the Library of Congress itself contains thousands of titles on the subject. This reflects, no doubt, the Constitution's seven articles and twenty-seven amendments being many things to many people—and any review of them nearly always invites debate. Our highest hopes for our graphic adaptation of the Constitution are to encourage awareness of the document and the issues that flow from it, and to add to that debate. During our own research, we found the following books particularly useful:

The Federalist, by Alexander Hamilton, James Madison, and John Jay
Our Constitution, by Donald A. Ritchie & JusticeLearning.org
America's Constitution: A Biography, by Akhil Reed Amar
Founding Brothers: The Revolutionary Generation, by Joseph J. Ellis
Magruder's American Government, by William A. McClenaghan
The Heritage Guide to the Constitution, by Edwin Meese III
The Summer of 1787: The Men Who Invented the Constitution, by David O. Stewart

Copies of the Constitution are readily available online. The Cornell University Law School's Legal Information Institute (www.law.cornell.edu) also provides resources for further study.

For more Web material, the National Constitution Center (www.constitutioncenter .org) offers great variety, including its "Digital Debates" podcasts.

ACKNOWLEDGMENTS

The first and deepest bow this book makes is to those who lived and died to create and defend the Constitution of the United States. They are first among equals to the people on both sides of the judge's bench who wrestle it toward its highest principles. And to the scholars who made the Constitution knowable and keep it that way, we'll say this book is a palimpsest.

To Frank Scatoni of Venture Literary, our hats are so far off our heads as to be in the ionosphere. Frank generously looked our way, thought he saw something, and did so much to fire up this book's ignition. Every writer and illustrator should be so lucky.

Thomas LeBien. Editor. We will hardly be the first to salute, among Thomas's virtues of intellect, tact, savvy, patience, and faith in education—and, yes, in books (writ large)—his true belief in the nonfiction graphic novel. Other editors, other publishers, would have been satisfied with a lot less. And we know it.

Elizabeth Maples was wonderful in her constant effort and attention. Thanks as well to Jeff Seroy and Kathy Daneman.

My involvement with this project might never have become a reality without the encouragement and support of Annie Oelschlager. And that goes, too, for Marne' Akal Moore, Shauna Cross, and my parents, Richard Hennessey and Lynne Hennessey.

In the thick of the writing and research, so many people were so quick to pitch in with their thoughts and expertise that one could have built a new faith in human nature, one brick at a time. So, all praise to folks like Mateo Barnstone, the capital of Virginia historian Mark Greenough, Darrin Pufall at the University of Portland, Mary Steffens at the office of Congressman David Dreier, and the staff of the Library of Congress.

Finally, I have to single out my partner, Aaron McConnell, whose talent is incredible to me. I get pangs when I image the blood, sweat, and tears he paid to this book. Thanks, too, to Jason Arthur and everyone else who pitched in on every step of production.

—*Jonathan Hennessey*

My thanks go out to Periscope Studio for assistance in finishing the artwork. I owe a lifetime's supply of VooDoo Donuts to Steve Lieber, who not only inked more than half the book and profoundly improved my pencils, but also kept my head above water with invaluable time-management strategies. A special thanks to the most unflappable interns a studio could wish for, Elaine Rogers and Jose A. Pimienta, who day after day added watercolors to page after page. Cat Ellis and James Ratcliffe not only added digital color, but also kept a positive aura of diligence and accomplishment in the studio comparable, I would like to imagine, to the energy of the Constitutional Convention. Other friends and studio members who helped include Dennis Culver, Gohma Schwartz, Jonathan Case, Colleen Coover, David Hahn, Jeff Parker, Susan Tardif, Ron Chan, Natalie Nourigat, Lee Moyer, Shane Nitzsche, Dylan Meconis, Jesse Hamm, Ron Randall, Karl Kesel, and Terri (The state bird of Utah is a seagull?!) Nelson.

I owe my wife, Ruby, and son, Alden, the world for supporting, loving, and tolerating me during this endeavor. (Sam Cooke's "Just for You" says it best.) My parents' enthusiasm for this project as well as every tiny little creative effort that lead me to this book have spoiled me rotten. "Thanks again" seems to cover all their unconditional love and support. My father helped save the day by applying his deft inks and watercolors to a number of pages within this book. Lastly, my undying thanks to Jonathan, who made every wrist cramp, back spasm, and sleepless night worth the effort by writing an inspirational adaptation that illuminates the humanity at the core of our Constitution.

—Aaron McConnell